— TechnoFeminism —

— TechnoFeminism —

JUDY WAJCMAN

polity

First published in 2004 by Polity Press.
Reprinted 2005, 2006

Polity Press
65 Bridge Street
Cambridge CB2 1UR, UK

Polity Press
350 Main Street
Malden, MA 02148, USA

A catalogue record for this book is available from the British Library.

Library of Congress Cataloging-in-Publication Data

Wajcman, Judy.
  TechnoFeminism / Judy Wajcman.
    p. cm.
    ISBN 0-7456-3043-X (hb : alk. paper) – ISBN 0-7456-3044-8
  (pb : alk. paper)
  1. Technology–Social aspects. 2. Sex role. 3. Women–Effect of
  technological innovations on. 4. Feminist theory. I. Title.
    HM846.W35 2004
    303.48'3–dc22

                                                        2003016990

Typeset in 11 on 13 pt Sabon
by SNP Best-set Typesetter Ltd., Hong Kong
Printed and bound in Great Britain by
Marston Book Services Limited, Oxford

For further information on Polity, visit our website: www.polity.co.uk

Contents

Preface

Over a decade ago I wrote *Feminism Confronts Technology*. That book made a strong case for building a feminist perspective into social science debates about technology. Taking an in-depth look at a whole range of technologies, each chapter considered the differential impact of technological change on women and men before turning the focus around to examine their social shaping of technology. That artefacts are themselves shaped by gender relations, meanings and identities was demonstrated – from refrigerators to contraceptives, from houses, cars and cities to word processors and weapons. The book thus explored the way hierarchies of sexual difference profoundly affect the design, development, diffusion and use of technologies.

TechnoFeminism is a continuation of the project. However, I have not attempted to traverse the same ground – that is, the full range of feminist scholarship on individual technologies. This would now be impossible to achieve in one slim volume. *Feminism Confronts Technology* can usefully be regarded as a companion volume to *TechnoFeminism*, providing as it does a wealth of historical and contemporary material that supports the overall argument.

The present book is more in the nature of an essay, in which I highlight the continuities and discontinuities between current and earlier feminist reflections on science and technology. Here I have purposely concentrated on the frontier technologies of information, communication and biomedicine. Both books are positioned at the intersection of feminist studies of technoscience and the field of science and technology studies (STS), where cross-fertilizations are inspiring new insights.

International feminist communities of technoscience scholars, as well as the network of the Society for Social Studies of Science (4S), have provided the context for writing this book. Many individuals have helped by discussing the ideas and commenting on drafts. My greatest debt as ever is to Jenny Earle. I also wish to thank Anne-Jorunn Berg, Danielle Chabaud-Rychter, John Holmwood, Lynn Jamieson, Martha Macintyre, Donald MacKenzie, Maureen McNeil, Stuart Rosewarne, Lucy Suchman and Dave Walsh. Ceridwen Roncelli provided excellent research assistance. I enjoyed stimulating exchanges with my colleagues and students at the Gender Institute, London School of Economics. For the increasingly scarce resource of time, I heartily thank the Research School of Social Sciences, Australian National University. Finally, I would like to thank John Thompson for suggesting that I write it.

Introduction: Feminist Utopia or Dystopia?

> She shot smoothly upwards. The very fabric of life now, she thought as she rose, is magic. In the eighteenth century, we knew how everything was done; but here I rise through the air; I listen to voices in America; I see men flying – but how it's done, I can't even begin to wonder. So my belief in magic returns.
>
> Virginia Woolf, *Orlando*

The urge to defy gravity has been a continuing impulse in our quest to transcend the natural world. The elevator, the telephone, the radio, and the aeroplane referred to by Virginia Woolf were the mysteries of modern technology in her day. Compared to people in earlier times, we rarely have a chance to live outside technology. More and more of life is somehow mediated by technology, so that today there is hardly any human activity that occurs without it. Yet it doesn't seem to have lost its mystery with familiarity. Nowadays, it is the rapidly evolving information and communication technologies that are experienced as magic, and evoke dreams and desires about the future.

For many, the global information society, characterized by the compression of space and time, marks a whole new epoch in the human condition. The nature of work, consumption and social interaction are all in a state of flux. There is much talk of the 'digital divide', between countries and within them, as the new source of inequality in the twenty-first century. The sheer rate of change in technoscience contributes to the pervasive late-modern sense of risk, insecurity and excitement. At the same time, new biomedical technologies that allow us to remodel the human body, profile individuals and populations, and commodify nature in unprecedented ways are changing the idea of what it means to be human, and even our sense of self. These developments call for some radical rethinking both of the processes of technological innovation and of their impact on the culture and practices of everyday life.

For everybody, technological change is the intractable fate of the world, an irreversible process. Frequently, the level of scientific and technological development is taken as the index of a society's advancement. Our icons of progress are drawn from science, technology and medicine; we revere that which is defined as 'rational', as distinct from that which is judged 'emotional'. Yet, as we enter the new millennium, we are no longer sure whether science and technology are the solution to the world's problems – such as environmental degradation, unemployment and war – or the cause of them. It is not surprising, therefore, that the relationship between technoscience and society is currently being subjected to profound and urgent questioning.

For women, whose lives have undergone massive transformation in the course of the last century, these questions are particularly vexed. Women's new-found economic independence, resulting from the feminization of the paid labour force, has been accompanied by a profound cultural shift and widespread public discourse about gender equity. A liberal commitment to equality between the sexes in both the public and the private spheres is now broadly accepted in Western societies, and is enshrined in law, even if substantial inequalities remain in practice. What it means to be a man or a woman is no longer ordained by 'nature' – gendered identities are contested terrain.

These dramatic social changes are associated with the unprecedented technological options available to us. Feminism has long been conflicted, however, about the impact of technology on women, torn between utopian and dystopian visions of what the future may hold. In both these scenarios, the future is crowded with automata, androids and robots. This fusion of technology with ideals, hopes and nightmares about the future has a venerable history. From Thomas More's original *Utopia* to Aldous Huxley's *Brave New World*, imaginary voyages and invented worlds, fantasies of timeless time and non-physical space, have been continuing themes in modern Western culture. Promises of emancipation from the frail-ties and failings of mortal flesh have reached a new crescendo in the cyberspace age. What might these imag-inings about the future reveal about contemporary gender relations? How does the social and political revolution in women's lives relate to the digital revolution?

Seen through one lens, virtual reality is a new space for undermining old social relations, a place of freedom and liberation from conventional gender roles. Cyberfeminists have coffee in cyber-cafes, surf the Internet, and imagine a gender-free future in cyberspace. Electronic networks offer women new possibilities for global information exchange and for participatory democracy. The influence of the anti-corporate globalization movement and NGO (non-governmental organization) activists is a testament to the effectiveness of the Internet for political mobiliza-tion. In this account, the World Wide Web is seen as beyond the control of any one group, and thus open to being deployed by women for their own social and politi-cal purposes. This is highly subversive of the conventional definition of women as biologically determined and con-fined to the private sphere. The twin visions of bodily tran-scendence in cyberspace and easy engagement in the public realm of international politics are certainly seductive.

Seen through another lens, the Internet is marked by its military origins and the white male hacker world that spawned it. The contemporary use of the Web by transnational corporations, financial markets, global criminal networks, military strategists and international racists is a means to evade social regulation, entrench political control, and concentrate economic power. Men still heavily dominate these institutions and groups, and there are dramatic gender differentials in access to, and control over, electronic networks. Furthermore, rather than celebrating cyberspace for providing the opportunity for free expression of people's desires, we should lament the massive growth of pornographic web sites, amongst the most frequently visited and most profitable sites on the Internet. Sexual harassment, the international sex trade, paedophile networks, and anxiety about children's vulnerability are the focus of this perspective.

Biomedical technologies are also the site of hopes and fears. These technologies appear to offer fantastic opportunities for self-realization – we can literally redesign our bodies and commission designer babies. Women can defy biology altogether by choosing not to have a child, choosing to have a child after menopause, or choosing the sex of their child. The ubiquitous cyborg has become an icon for the idea that the boundaries between the biological and the cultural, and between the human and the machine, have been dissolved. These dichotomies situated women as natural and different, and served to sustain the previously ordained gender order. Severing the link between femininity and maternity, as these new body technologies do, disrupts the categories of the body, sex, gender and sexuality. This is liberating for women, who have been captive to biology.

At the same time, there is the spectre of genetic engineering and cloning depriving women of any control over reproduction. In this apocalyptic view, technoscience is deeply implicated in the masculine project of the domination and control of women and nature. The classic trope of science fiction, Frankenstein and his monster, is invoked as the dark side of the cyborg – artificial life out of control. Fears abound about how knowledge of the genome will be used to intervene in and redesign nature, whether it be genetically modified foods, cloned animals or perfectly bred human beings. Life itself (human, plant and animal) is at risk of becoming biomedicalized and commodified. Genetic and reproductive engineering, then, are regarded as another attempt to usurp self-determination of women's bodies.

Images of women's prospects in the digital economy are also widely divergent. For some, the expansion of the information-intensive service sector is producing a society based on lifelong learning and a knowledge economy. The dominant form of work becomes based on expertise, judgement and discretion, requiring employees with high levels of skills and knowledge. Women will be at an advantage because service work increasingly utilizes the feminine aptitudes for communication and social skills. Similarly, women managers will be ideally suited to post-industrial corporations that increasingly require the more empathetic, 'soft' co-operative styles of management. One might conclude that the future of work is female.

This future can also be depicted as a proliferation of flexible, temporary and contingent jobs for women. Work in the new economy is typified by call centres and fast food establishments, involving simple, routine, predictable tasks requiring little skill from those who perform them. Contemporary computerized workplaces provide enhanced tools for electronic surveillance and monitoring of employees' performance. Far from a family-friendly option, telework exacerbates women's domestic burden and the intensification of work. Furthermore, the spatial flexibility afforded by information and communication technologies allows firms to shift a growing range of tasks offshore, to take advantage of low-cost female labour in developing countries. Accordingly, new forms of work in the knowledge economy replicate old patterns of exploitation and sex segregation in the labour market.

How do we make sense of such radically different interpretations of the same phenomena? Is there an alternative to the limited options of simply rejecting existing technologies or uncritically embracing technological change? Can feminism steer a path between technophobia and technophilia? This book provides an opportunity to explore the complex ways in which women's everyday lives and technological change interrelate in the age of digitalization. My aim is to offer a way between utopian optimism and pessimistic fatalism for technofeminism, and between cultural contingency and social determinism in social theory.

The book begins with an overview of early attempts by feminist scholars to understand the link between technology and gender. Much of the literature discussed in this first chapter is concerned to explain men's historical hold on machines and the continuing under-representation of women in scientific and technological fields. The core argument here is that technology is a key source of men's power and a defining feature of masculinity. This approach served as a compelling critique of popular and sociological arguments that were, and still are, characterized by technological determinism. In this context, however, initial theories about the impact of technology on women's lives often took the form of an essentialist account of gender, and an over-determined analysis of patriarchal technology. Technology may have been seen as socially shaped, but shaped by men to the exclusion of women. I argue that this generated a rather pessimistic view, one that emphasized the role of technology in reproducing the gendered division of labour.

With the emergence of radically new technologies, contemporary feminist debates have been much more optimistic about the possibilities that are opening up for women. At the same time, a fresh and increasingly sophisticated perspective known as the social studies of science and technology has evolved. The fruitful interchange between gender theory and developments in science and technology studies is explored in chapter 2. As a result of the cross-fertilization, feminists have drawn on and reconfigured sociological theories that treat technology as a sociotechnical product – that is, as shaped in the social relations that produce and use it. We have begun to conceive of a mutually shaping relationship between gender and technology, in which technology is both a source and a consequence of gender relations. This is what I will describe as the emerging *technofeminist* framework. An emphasis on the contingency and heterogeneity of technological change helps to locate its possibilities in wider social networks. Such an analysis introduces space for women's agency in transforming technologies.

Into this space came cyberfeminism. The cultural turn against determinist arguments, emphasizing subjectivity and agency, generates a utopian perspective. This is particularly characteristic of post-feminist cultural theories of technology, the subject of the third chapter. A common argument here is that the digital revolution heralds the decline of traditional institutional practices and power bases – including patriarchal power. The virtuality of cyberspace is seen to spell the end of naturalized, biological embodiment as the basis for gender difference. The Internet is expressive of female ways of being, and thereby creates manifold opportunities for changing the woman–machine relationship. Technology itself is seen as liberating women.

While many have been drawn to cyberfeminism, it is the cyborg figure that has most strongly fired the feminist imagination. This can be understood as a reaction, on the one hand, to feminist theories that treat women as passive victims of technological change and, on the other, to those that see new technical forms as offering unlimited freedom. This reflects an enduring division within feminist theory. The appeal of Donna Haraway's work on the prosthetic possibilities of biotechnologies lies in its bold attempt to bridge these polarized positions. The fourth chapter will assess Haraway's 'material-semiotic' approach and discuss the myriad ways in which her work has been taken up and popularized. It will explore the ramifications of what I will refer to as the 'cyborg solution'. I argue that while Haraway's work has stimulated important new insights into the gender power relations of technology, she too – but even more so her acolytes – risk fetishizing new technologies.

The technofeminist approach I outline in the final chapter fuses the insights of cyborg feminism with those of the social shaping, or constructivist, theory of technology. I reflect on what technofeminism means both for analytical arguments and for politics. The old discourse of sex difference has been made increasingly untenable by the dramatic changes in technology, by the challenge of feminism, and by awareness of the mutating character of the natural world. A recognition that gender and technoscience are mutually constitutive opens up fresh possibilities for feminist scholarship and action. Engagement with the process of technical change must be part of the renegotiation of gender power relations.

I take this as my central concern, while fully recognizing that gender is not the only axis of social hierarchy and identity (just as there are sites not primarily marked by gender). Indeed, the enormous variability in gendering by place, nationality, class, race, ethnicity, sexuality and generation makes a nuanced exploration of the similarities and differences between and across women's and men's experience of technoscience all the more necessary. In referring to technofeminism, rather than technofeminism*s*, then, I do not mean to imply a consensus, but rather a coming together of many diverse voices engaged in dialogue, influencing each other and each being modified in the process.

Revolutions in technology do not create new societies, but they do change the terms in which social, political and economic relations are played out. Feminist theory offers a long tradition of analysing the gendered effects of the power to define, to make distinctions, and to literally build worlds. It is a tribute to the richness of the feminist enterprise that such analysis continues to be extended to new fields of inquiry. Technoscience as a gendered domain is now firmly within our sights. This book is intended as a contribution to that project.

− 1 −

Male Designs on Technology

Technology is a medium of power.
Cynthia Cockburn, *Machinery of Dominance*

In their 'millennial' reflections on the end of the twentieth century and the beginning of the twenty-first, many social scientists as well as popular commentators see technology as providing the impetus for the most fundamental of social trends and transformations. Indeed, understanding the role of technologies in the economy and society is now central to social theory. While there are a variety of social theories that proclaim the radical transformation of society, all contain, at their core, claims about technological change and its social impact. This is as true of the three paradigmatic theories of the transformation that Western societies are undergoing − the theories of the information society, post-Fordism and postmodernity − as it is of more recent theories of globalization. Much emphasis is placed on major new clusters of scientific and technological innovations, particularly the widespread use of information and communications technologies and the convergence of technologically mediated ways of life around the globe.

According to globalization gurus such as Anthony Giddens and Manuel Castells, states and societies across the world are experiencing historically unprecedented change as they try to adapt to a more interconnected but highly uncertain world.[1] Prominence is given to the intensity, extensity and velocity of global flows, interactions and networks embracing all social domains. In the 'information society' or 'knowledge economy', the dominant form of work becomes information- and knowledge-based. At the same time leisure, education, family relationships and personal identities are seen as moulded by the pressures exerted by, and opportunities arising from, the new technical forces. For these writers, such changes entail the breakup of hierarchical arrangements and herald a new post-traditional network society.

These ideas – or ideas like them – are now commonplace in sociology, and I foreground them here to illustrate the centrality of technology to contemporary theories of social, cultural and economic change. There are strong echoes of the earlier 'post-industrial society' thesis in these accounts, and its tendency to adopt a technologically determinist stance.[2] At that time, it was suggested that the industrial economy of manufacturing and factory production was being displaced by knowledge work. The old hierarchies of manual work would be replaced by more open and negotiated relationships.

Much critical writing at the time took issue with the idea of a post-industrial society, but with hindsight we can see that some of the underlying trends in the economy were well captured. The recent return to ideas of an information society and knowledge economy attests to this. Post-industrial theorists concentrated on hierarchies of class, rather than those of gender and, like their predecessors, the new theorists of technology also fail to consider whether this technological revolution might have a differential impact on women and men. While the common theme is that everything in the digital future will be different, it is not clear if the social relations of gender will also be different because the question is seldom raised. While the optimistic commentators on the digital revolution promise freedom, empowerment and wealth, rarely do they show any consciousness of the relationship between technology and gender. They seem oblivious to the fact that men still dominate scientific and technological fields and institutions. To be in command of the very latest technology signifies a greater involvement in, if not power over, the future.

It is no accident that the debates over post-industrialism coincided with the re-emergence to prominence of feminism. Clearly, profound social changes were under way in this period. But where post-industrial theorists were generally optimistic about the implications of technological change, second-wave feminism, and the growing body of feminist scholarship that flourished with it, identified women's absence from these spheres of influence as a key feature of gender power relations. By ignoring this axis of inequality, mainstream social theorists missed a central dynamic of technological development. It is being missed, once again, in contemporary social theory.

This chapter charts the growth of a gender perspective on technology. Feminists have identified men's monopoly of technology as an important source of their power; women's lack of technological skills as an important element in their dependence on men. Whilst there is broad agreement on this issue, the question whether the problem lies in men's monopoly of technology or whether technology itself is inherently patriarchal remains more contentious.

Feminist theories of the relationship between gender and technology have taken diverse forms. While liberal feminism conceived of the problem as one of equality of access and opportunity, socialist and radical feminism analysed the gendered nature of technology itself. The social factors that shape different technologies came under scrutiny, especially the way technology reflects gender divisions and inequalities. This approach served as a compelling critique of popular and sociological arguments that were, and still are, characterized by technological determinism. However, although coming from fundamentally different perspectives, early feminist analyses of technology tended to generate a fatalism that emphasized the role of technology in reproducing patriarchy. As we shall see, it is this pessimism that needs to be modified in the light of more recent arguments about new technologies, whilst building on the rich contribution of this earlier feminist literature.

From Access to Equity

Interest in gender, science and technology arose out of the contemporary women's movement and a general concern for women's position in the professions. Since the early 1970s, the publication of biographical studies of great women scientists has served as a useful corrective to mainstream histories of science in demonstrating that women have in fact made important contributions to scientific endeavour. The biographies of Rosalind Franklin and Barbara McClintock are probably the best-known examples.[3] Recovering the history of women's achievements became an integral part of feminist scholarship in a wide range of disciplines. Thanks to this work, we now know that during the industrial era women invented or contributed to the invention of such crucial machines as the cotton gin, the sewing machine, the small electric motor, the McCormick reaper and the Jacquard loom.[4] It has also been established that women played a major part in the early development of computers – a story that is still emerging from the recesses of Second World War history. However, as the extent and seemingly intransigent quality of women's exclusion from technoscience became more apparent, the approach gradually shifted from looking at exceptional women to examining the general patterns of women's participation.

Documenting and explaining women's limited access to scientific and technical institutions and careers was a major concern. Many studies identified the structural barriers to women's participation, looking at sex discrimination in employment and the kind of socialization and education that girls receive which channel them away from studying mathematics and science. Schooling, youth cultures, the family and the mass media all transmit meanings and values that identify masculinity with machines and technological competence. Sex stereotyping in schools was exposed, particularly the processes by which girls and boys are channelled into different subjects in secondary and tertiary education, and the link between education and the segregated labour market. Explaining the under-representation of women in science education, laboratories and scientific publications, research highlighted the construction and character of femininity encouraged by our culture.

Feminism in the 1970s and 1980s posed the solution in terms of getting more women to enter science and technology – seeing the issue as one of equal access to education and employment. Rather than questioning technoscience itself, it was generally assumed that science is intrinsically open, concerned with unbiased and objective research. If girls were given the right opportunities and encouragement, they could easily become scientists and engineers. Remedying the gender deficit was seen as a problem that could be overcome by a combination of different socialization processes and equal opportunity policies.

This liberal feminist tradition locates the problem in women (their socialization, their aspirations and values) and does not ask the broader questions of whether, and in what way, technoscience and its institutions could be reshaped to accommodate women. The equal opportunity recommendations, moreover, ask women to exchange major aspects of their gender identity for a masculine version without prescribing a similar 'degendering' process for men. For example, the current career structure for a professional scientist dictates long unbroken periods of intensive study and research that simply do not allow for child care and domestic responsibilities. In order to succeed, women have to model themselves on men who have traditionally avoided such commitments.

The equal opportunities strategy has had limited success precisely because it fails to challenge the sexual division of labour in the wider society. Women's reluctance 'to enter' is to do with the sex-stereotyping of technology as an activity appropriate for men. As with science, the very language of technology, its symbolism, is masculine. It is not simply a question of acquiring skills, because these skills are embedded in a culture of masculinity that is largely coterminous with the culture of technology. Both at school and in the workplace this culture is incompatible with femininity. Therefore, to enter this world, to learn its language, women have first to forsake their femininity.

Indeed, the very definition of technology is cast in terms of male activities. We tend to think about technology in terms of industrial machinery and cars, for example, ignoring other technologies that affect most aspects of everyday life. The history of technology still represents the prototype inventor as male.

However, the concept of technology is itself subject to historical change, and different epochs and cultures had different names for what we now think of as technology. A greater emphasis on women's activities immediately suggests that women, and in particular indigenous women, were amongst the first technologists. After all, women were the main gatherers, processors and storers of plant food from earliest human times onward. It is therefore logical that they should be the ones to have invented the tools and methods involved in this work, such as the digging stick, the carrying sling, the reaping knife and sickle, pestles and pounders. The male orientation of most technological research has long obscured the significance of 'women's sphere' inventions, and this in turn has served to reinforce the cultural stereotype of technology as an activity appropriate for men.

Indeed, it was only with the formation of engineering as a white, male, middle-class profession that 'male machines rather than female fabrics' became the modern markers of technology.[5] During the late nineteenth century mechanical and civil engineering increasingly came to define what technology is, diminishing the significance of both artefacts and forms of knowledge associated with women. This was the result of the rise of engineers as an elite with exclusive rights to technical expertise. Crucially, it involved the creation of a male professional identity, based on educational qualifications and the promise of managerial positions, sharply distinguished from shop-floor engineering and blue-collar workers. It also involved an ideal of manliness, characterized by the cultivation of bodily prowess and individual achievement. The discourse about manliness was mobilized to ensure that class, race and gender boundaries were drawn around the engineering bastion. It was during and through this process that the term 'technology' took on its modern meaning. Whereas the earlier concept of useful arts had included needlework and metalwork as well as spinning and mining, by the 1930s this had been supplanted by the idea of technology as applied science. At the same time, femininity was being reinterpreted as incompatible with technological pursuits. The legacy of this relatively recent history is our taken-for-granted association of technology with men.

Science as Ideology

Much early second-wave feminism then, was, of a liberal cast, demanding access for women within existing power structures, including technoscience. Feminist writing in this vein focused on gender stereotypes and customary expectations, and denied the existence of sex differences between women and men. It was based on an empiricist view of science and technology as fundamentally (gender) neutral. Sexism and androcentrism were understood as social biases capable of correction by stricter adherence to the methodological norms of scientific inquiry. The problem was framed in terms of the uses and abuses to which science and technology has been put by men.

The radical political movements of the late 1960s and early 1970s also began with this outlook. Research and campaigns depicted an abusing, militarized and polluting technoscience, directed towards profit and warfare. Initially science itself was seen as neutral or value-free, and potentially useful as long as it was in the hands of those working for a just society. Gradually, however, the radical science movement developed a Marxist analysis of the class character of science and its links with capitalist methods of production. A revived political economy of science argued that the growth and nature of modern science were related to the needs of capitalist society. Increasingly tied to the state and industry, science had become directed towards domination. The idea that science is neutral was seen as an ideology with a specific historical development. One of the characteristic formulations of this position, associated with the radical science movement, was that 'science is social relations'. The point was that the distinction between science and ideology could not be sustained because the dominant social relations of society at large are constitutive of science.

Despite the recognition that scientific knowledge is profoundly affected by the society in which it is conducted, gender-conscious accounts were rare. The women's health movement that developed in America and Britain during the 1970s provided an important impetus to the emergence of a feminist politics about scientific knowledge. Campaigns for improved birth control and abortion rights were central to the early period of second-wave feminism. They challenged the growth and consolidation of male expertise at the expense of both women's health and women's healing skills. Regaining knowledge and control over women's bodies – their sexuality and fertility – was seen as crucial to women's liberation.

The women's health, peace and environmental movements all initially saw science as alien and opposed to
women's interests. This was in particular a reaction to
the way biology and medical science had cast women as
different and inferior, and made a case for biologically
determined sex roles. By the 1980s, feminist criticisms of
science had, in Sandra Harding's words, evolved from
asking the 'woman question' in science to asking the more
radical 'science question' in feminism.[6] Rather than asking
how women can be more equitably treated within and by
science, feminist critics asked how a science apparently so
deeply involved in distinctively masculine projects could
possibly be used for emancipatory ends. Western science
was characterized as a masculine project of reason and
objectivity, with women relegated to nature rather than
culture. Rejecting scientific knowledge as patriarchal
knowledge, there were calls for the development of a new
science based on women's values.

At the same time, feminist analyses of technology were
shifting beyond the approach of 'women and technology'
to examine the very processes whereby technology is
developed and used, as well as those whereby gender is
constituted. In other words, feminists were exploring the
gendered character of technology itself. This approach has
broadly taken two directions: one influenced by radical
feminism, the other identified with socialist feminism.

Technology as Patriarchal

The view that Western technology itself embodies patriarchal values, and that its project is the domination and
control of women and nature, is an important precept of
radical feminism, cultural feminism and eco-feminism.
These feminisms emphasize gender difference and celebrate what they see as specifically feminine, such as
women's greater humanism, pacifism, nurturance and spiritual development. The idea that what is specifically fem-

inine is socially produced was abandoned, and notions of ineradicable difference flourished. This approach has been particularly influential in relation to the technologies of human biological reproduction. It is fuelled by the perception that the processes of pregnancy and childbirth are directed and controlled by ever more sophisticated and intrusive technologies. Radical feminists' strong opposition to the development of the new reproductive technologies reflects fears of patriarchal exploitation of women's bodies. Central to this analysis is a concept of reproduction as a natural process, inherent in women alone, and a theory of technology as an agent of patriarchy.

In the early period of the contemporary women's movement, by contrast, reproductive technology was seen as particularly progressive because it opened up the potential for finally severing the link between sexuality and reproduction. The much-cited advocate of the use of high technology to liberate women was Shulamith Firestone. In *The Dialectic of Sex* she emphasized the need to develop effective contraceptive and birth technologies in order to free women from the 'tyranny of reproduction' which dictated the nature of women's oppression.[7] Patriarchy was seen to be fundamentally about the control of women's bodies, especially their sexuality and fertility, by men. This view located women's oppression in their own biology and posited a technological fix in the shape of ectogenesis. The application of a neutral technology would bring an end to biological motherhood and thus make sexual equality possible.

Firestone's enthusiasm for the artificial womb as the key to women's liberation was not shared by the growing feminist opposition to the development and application of genetic and reproductive engineering. Most vocal were the group of radical feminists known as FINRRAGE (Feminist International Network of Resistance to Reproductive and Genetic Engineering), who saw the development of reproductive technologies as a form of patriarchal exploitation of women's bodies.[8] Whereas Firestone saw women's reproductive role as the source of their oppression, FINRRAGE writers reclaimed the experience of motherhood as the foundation of women's identity, as 'the qualities of mothering or maternal thinking stand in opposition to the destructive, violent and self-aggrandizing characteristics of men'.[9]

The technological potential for the complete separation of reproduction from sexuality, celebrated by Firestone, was now seen as an attack on women. For this group of feminists, techniques such as *in vitro* fertilization, egg donation, sex predetermination and embryo evaluation offered a powerful means of social control because they would become standard practice. Just as obstetric procedures were first introduced for 'high-risk' cases but are now used routinely on most birthing women, these authors feared that the new techniques would eventually be used on a large proportion of the female population. Radical feminist theory sees these techniques as an attempt to appropriate the reproductive capacities that have been, in the past, women's unique source of power.

The most powerful statement of this was Gena Corea's image of 'the reproductive brothel' which extrapolates from the way animals are now used like machines to breed, to a future in which women will become professional breeders, 'the mother machine' at men's command. Some writers argued that these techniques would actually replace natural reproduction, guaranteeing the fabrication of genetically perfect babies. According to this futuristic dystopia, men will achieve ultimate control of human creation and women will become redundant (this is an argument that has its parallel in current popular worries about the future of men in an increasingly feminized workforce).

FINRRAGE saw reproductive technologies as inextricably linked with genetic engineering and eugenics. A parallel was drawn between the way men have been increasingly controlling the reproduction of animals to improve their stock by experimenting on them and the extension of this form of experimentation to women. The female body is being expropriated, fragmented and dissected as raw material, or treated as a 'living laboratory' as Renate Klein puts it, for the technological production of human beings. Their arguments were prescient. It is techniques such as *in vitro* fertilization that provide researchers with the embryo material on which to do scientific research, particularly stem cell research. However, these critics underestimated the extent to which women's demands for the new reproductive technologies would be crucial in fostering their development.

Embedded in the radical feminist approach is a conception of technoscience as intrinsically patriarchal. For example, Maria Mies argued that it makes absolutely no difference whether it is women or men who apply and control this technology; this technology is in itself an instrument of domination, 'a new stage in the patriarchal war against women'. Technology is not neutral but is always based on 'exploitation of and domination over nature, exploitation and subjection of women, exploitation and oppression of other peoples'.[10] Mies argued that this is the very logic of the natural sciences and its model is the machine. For her the method of technical progress is the violent destruction of natural links between living organisms, the dissection and analysis of these organisms down to their smallest elements, in order to reassemble them, according to the plans of the male engineers, as machines. Reproductive and genetic technologies are about conquering the 'last frontier' of men's domination over nature.

In a similar vein, eco-feminists analysed military technology and the ecological effects of other modern technologies as products of a violent patriarchal culture. Technology, like science, is seen as an instrument of male domination of women and nature. After the Scientific Revolution, Western culture ceased to view the earth as an organism to be nurtured and instead treats nature as a machine to be exploited in the name of progress. The mechanical framework, with its associated values of abstract reason, order and control, sanctioned the management of both nature and society. The eco-feminist critique identified the harnessing of technology as fostering domination and, as Rachel Carson highlighted, as potentially destructive to the health of communities.[11] Above all, the critique pointed to technology as the instrument for reorganizing the modes of interaction with the natural environment. In the process, nature would be called into the service of mankind, with men established as producers, women recast as the 'hewers of wood' and 'fetchers of water', men bequeathed the benefits of nature's bounty and women's labours marginalized and made more onerous.

This was an order that eco-feminists demanded be challenged. Mythologizing the past, women's biology and nature were celebrated as the source of a female power that could resist male technology. Drawing on this, a new feminist technoscience would be built on the vitality and fecundity of womanhood and nature; feminine intuition and an ethics of caring and responsibility would lay the foundations for a non-exploitative relationship between nature and humanity.

Radical feminism, cultural feminism and eco-feminism had a very positive impact on the debate about gender and technology, taking it beyond the use/misuse model and focusing on the political qualities of technology itself. These approaches were a forceful assertion of women's interests and needs as being different from men's and highlighted the way in which women are not always well served by current technologies. They also contributed to a much more sophisticated debate about women's exclusion from the processes of innovation and from the acquisition of technical skills. Where liberal feminism saw power in terms of relations between individual people, radical feminism emphasized the way in which power was embedded more deeply within social structures. Throughout this book I will argue that certain kinds of technology are inextricably linked to particular institutionalized patterns of power and authority, and the case of reproductive technologies is no exception. If we regard technology as neutral, but subject to possible misuse, we will be blinded to the consequences of artefacts being designed and developed in particular ways that embody gendered power relations.

A common problem in radical feminism, however, was its tendency to essentialism, representing women as inherently nurturing and pacifist. These ideas have been subjected to a variety of critiques both within and without these approaches. They overlook the role of culture and history in shaping women's needs and priorities in different contexts, ignoring the way women's experience is divided by class, race and sexuality. In this way, they portray women as uniformly victims of patriarchal technoscience. Too often the result is a pessimistic account of the role of technoscience as determining women's fate, as men gain more control over our bodies. Although the idea of a technology based on *women's* values has lost much of its salience, the idea of a technology based upon *different* values remains a valid concern, a point to which we return in chapter 5.

Sex, Class and Technology

Whereas radical feminism focused on women's bodies/ sexuality, the core concern of socialist feminism was the relationship between technology and women's work – both paid and unpaid. The changes in this area during the second half of the twentieth century have indeed been revolutionary. In the West there was a major shift in employment from factory work to service industries and office work, and this was accompanied by the feminization of the labour force which gave women new-found economic independence. The introduction of computer-based technologies into offices became a prime site for socialist feminist research, because the majority of clerical and secretarial workers almost everywhere were women. This research examined the effects of technological change on women's employment opportunities, their experience of work, and their skills. The exploitation of Third World women as a source of cheap labour for the manufacture of computers, then theorized as the 'new international division of labour' (in contrast to today's rather bland catch-all term 'globalization'), was also scrutinized.[12]

Then, as now, starkly opposed views were expressed about the effects of office automation. While both sides recognized that the traditional secretarial job was becoming obsolete, with the word processor replacing the typewriter, optimists writing about the coming of post-industrial society predicted that these jobs would be replaced by different types of para-professional jobs. Routine typing would be minimized, releasing the office-worker to take on more skilled, satisfying work, as well as more responsible duties. Technological advances would improve the quality of work, reducing drudgery and promoting more integrated work processes. In sum, automation would increase the skill requirements of existing jobs as well as creating many more highly skilled jobs. This vision attached great significance to the liberating potential of new office technologies, seeing in them a solution to women's traditionally limited and limiting work opportunities.

More common among socialist feminist writers, however, was a pessimistic view of the impact of microelectronic technology on women's work, often expressed in a strongly anti-technology stance. An initial concern was with the implications for women's health and safety of widespread use of video display terminals, from eye strain and headaches to the risks of radiation for pregnant women. More generally, there were fears that computerization of office work would lead to a huge reduction in the number of office jobs and the emergence of the 'paperless office'. Word processors were seen as a threat to typists' skills, which were being incorporated into the new machines. Secretarial work for those few who remained would be increasingly deskilled, fragmented into routine, standardized tasks, and subject to the control of the machine. With this rationalization of the office, the conditions of white-collar work would become increasingly like factory work, hence the term the 'proletarianization' of white-collar workers.

To understand the salience of this approach, we need to look at the framework that influenced its development. Like many of my feminist contemporaries, I came to gender and technology studies from having been immersed (in the 1970s) in Marxist labour process debates about production. Labour process analysis was especially critical of versions of Marxism in which the development of technology and productivity was seen as the motor force of history. These interpretations represented technology as beyond class struggle. The publication of Harry Braverman's *Labor and Monopoly Capital*, and the debate that ensued, restored Marx's critique of technology and the division of labour to the centre of his analysis of the process of capitalist development.[13] At the same time, the arguments could be directed against the optimistic scenarios of technological change presented by theorists of post-industrial society.

Labour process theorists criticized technological determinism, arguing that, far from constituting an autonomous force determining the organization of work, technology is itself crucially affected by the antagonistic class relations of production. In order to control the labour force and maximize profitability, capitalism continuously applies new technology designed to fragment and deskill labour, so that labour becomes cheaper and subject to greater control. Technological revolution was understood to be a trait of capital accumulation processes. Although this theoretical approach was sophisticated in its analysis of the capital–labour relation, feminists questioned the notion that control over the labour process could operate independently of the gender of the workers who were being controlled.

This, for me, was where the socialist feminist project began, as a critique of the gender-blindness of Marxism. Socialist feminist work pointed out that the division of labour characterizing paid occupations was a sexual hierarchy, and that its gendered nature was not incidental. A crucial historical perspective was brought to bear on the analysis of men's monopoly hold on technology. Extensive feminist research demonstrated that women's exclusion from technology was a consequence of the male domination of skilled trades that developed during the Industrial Revolution. Craft-workers, typically seen as the defenders of working-class interests in disputes over technical change, resisted the entry of women into skilled technical jobs in order to protect their own conditions.[14] Industrial technology from its origins thus reflected male power, as well as capitalist domination.

A classic socialist feminist study of the time was Cynthia Cockburn's *Brothers: Male Dominance and Technological Change*.[15] A history of typesetting technology in Britain, it describes how the employers' desire to deskill the workforce underpinned the development of new technology, and how its application took place in a context of intense struggles by print workers to retain their craft monopoly over the job. Rather than resisting mechanization, the male compositors (typesetters) fought instead to retain sole rights to the new equipment. Their success entailed the exclusion of unskilled women from the trade. Indeed the QWERTY keyboard of typewriters had been explicitly chosen over the traditional linotype keyboard as a strategy both to deskill men and to make it possible for lower-paid women to enter the workforce. Cockburn shows how printers perceived clashes over technological innovation as affecting not only the balance of power between capital and labour, but also as an aspect of gender power. The compositors' craft involved the construction of an identity both as skilled workers and as men. The two elements were inextricably linked. They experienced the move from hot metal linotype typesetting to cold computerized photocomposition as an affront to their masculinity, and they organized against it as though their virility depended on it. Here was a concrete demonstration of the mutual formation of class and gender.

Such studies of the relationship between skilled work, technology and masculinity provided a number of valuable insights.[16] They exposed the limitations of labour process theory's exclusive focus on class conflict in determining the effects of technical change on the workplace. The relations of production are constructed as much out of gender divisions as out of class divisions. Both employers as employers, and men as men, were shown to have an interest in creating and sustaining occupational sex segregation. Gender was shown time and time again to be an important factor in shaping the organization of work that results from technological change.

Further, men's traditional monopoly of technology has been identified as key to maintaining the definition of skilled work as men's work. The association between technology, masculinity, and the very notion of what constitutes skilled work is still fundamental to the way in which the gender division of labour is being reproduced today. Machine-related skills and physical strength are basic measures of masculine status and self-esteem, and by implication the least technical jobs are suitable for women. The result is that machinery is literally designed by men with men in mind – the masculinity of the technology becomes embedded in the technology itself.[17]

And if the workplace technology was patriarchal, then what about the domestic sphere? Feminists pointed out that the labour process as defined in mainstream work ignored a significant part of all labour – the unpaid labour done by women in the home. Women's unpaid work in the home, servicing men, children and other dependants, had for a long time been seen by feminists as a key to women's subordination. Considerable optimism had attached to the view that technology might provide the solution to the drudgery of housework. Feminist interest in domestic

technology can be traced back to this debate about housework as a key element of women's oppression. By the
1970s, housework was recognized as 'work' and had
become the object of serious academic study by historians
and sociologists.[18] Such research challenged the main orientation within the sociology of technology towards paid,
productive labour in the public domain. Marxist feminists,
myself included, argued that paid work could not be
understood without reference to women's unpaid work in
the home, and that the sexual division of labour separated
women from control over the technologies they utilized
both in the workplace and at home.

Dominating the debates was the apparent paradox
that mechanization of the home had not substantially
decreased the amount of time women spent on household
tasks. This discussion was fuelled by the early research on
domestic technology of feminist historians working in
North America.[19] Their studies analyse the relationship
between domestic technologies and the time spent on
household labour, examining whether technology has
affected the degree of gender specialization of housework,
as well as gender bias in the use of new technologies.

The central theme of Ruth Schwartz Cowan's *More
Work for Mother* was the failure of the 'industrial revolution in the home' to eliminate household tasks.[20] She
pointed to the contradictions inherent in attempts to mech-
anize the home and standardize domestic production. Such
attempts foundered on the nature of housework – privatized, decentralized and labour-intensive. The result is a
completely 'irrational' use of technology and labour within
the home, because of the dominance of single-family resi-
dences and the private ownership of correspondingly
small-scale amenities. Domestic technologies thus reflect
the sexual division of domestic activities and the social
organization of the family.

The lasting contribution of these approaches was to
bring the public/private distinction to the centre of critical
attention. Much social-scientific writing had addressed the

public spheres of work and politics as being of fundamental importance, and as separate from domestic relations. The latter were relegated to a less important private sphere. Men's experience was unreflectively regarded as the norm. Throughout the period, feminists showed how the public and the private were mutually formed and, thus, how gender was fundamental to all aspects of social life. Socialist feminist writers demonstrated the powerful interdependencies between the sexual division of labour at home and at work. Rather than being a consequence only of family socialization, masculine and feminine identities were produced and reproduced through all social relationships.

Conclusion

In this chapter, I have set out the major preoccupations of feminist scholars writing on technology in the early phases of this debate. New cross-disciplinary research areas were charted in order to counter the masculine bias in various academic subjects and the invisibility of women's lives. Feminism was concerned to show what being a woman might imply, and how women's lives were shaped by various social forces. The point was to identify major areas of gender inequality and oppression, and to seek to change them.

Such engagement with the realities of gendered structures of power inevitably gave rise to a sense of frustration. The tendency of these different schools of feminism was to see these structures as monolithic. In the rush to expose the depth and extent of men's technopower, they overlooked the subversive possibilities that may be opened up by new forms of technology, and the possibilities for destabilizing patriarchal structures. Technology was seen as an extension of patriarchal and capitalist domination. As a result, feminist approaches mainly dismissed technoscience as inherently patriarchal and malignant.

There has been much criticism of the all too common tendency to treat women as the passive victims of

technology.[21] While this determinism was more characteristic of radical feminism than of socialist feminism, traces
of this inheritance are evident in my book *Feminism Confronts Technology*. Although clearly critical of a radical or
eco-feminist position, which rejects technology in favour
of a return to a mythical natural state, the general tone is
rather negative about the possibilities of redesigning technologies for gender equality. Technology is seen as socially
shaped, but shaped by men to the exclusion of women.
The proclivity of technological developments to entrench
gender hierarchies is emphasized, rather than the prospects
they afford for change. In short, not enough attention is
paid to women's agency.

For all its limitations, it is clear that this body of literature was asking the right questions and was influential in
setting a very productive feminist research agenda. This
intellectual project was an emanation of second-wave feminism, as was the associated political project of building
women's technical knowledge and expertise.

The pessimism evident in many of the approaches I have
discussed contrasts with the optimism of general arguments about technological change associated with post-
industrial arguments of the past. With recent developments
of cyberspace and digital technologies, this optimism is to
the fore once again, with arguments about a networked
knowledge society. We do need to address current technoscience with a sensibility different from that which has
informed feminist attitudes to science and technology in
the past. That is what I shall do in the rest of the book.
But we should not lose sight of the issues of power and
constraint identified by an earlier generation of feminists.
Pessimism is a useful antidote to uncritical celebration.

For all the rhetoric about women prospering in the
emerging digital economy, all the signs are that men's domination of science and technology has continued. Women
are making few inroads into technology-related courses in
the information technology, electronics and communications sector, and face considerable barriers when they

attempt to pursue a professional or managerial career in
this sector. Indeed, the number of women with under-
graduate degrees in computer science in the USA nearly
halved between 1984 and 1999.[22] The result is that women
are chronically under-represented in precisely the jobs that
are key to the creation and design of technical systems in
the new economy. Increasingly, these technical systems
comprise the world we inhabit.

The connection between masculinity and technology,
reflected in women's under-representation in engineering,
and indeed in all scientific and technical institutions,
remains strong as we enter a new era of technological
change.

– 2 –

Technoscience Reconfigured

Men and things exchange properties and replace one
another; this is what gives technological projects their
full savour.

Bruno Latour, Aramis

Feminist approaches of the 1990s and today adopt an optimistic perspective on the nature of digital technologies and
their implications for women. In doing so, they present an
image of new technology as radically distinct from older
technologies and, as such, positive for women. In looking
forward to what these new technologies may make possible, they elaborate a new feminist 'imaginary' different
from the 'material reality' of the existing technological
order. In this way, in common with other proponents of
the impact of information and biotechnologies, they distinguish new technologies from more established ones, and
downplay any continuities between them.

While attributing a technological determinism to the
past, paradoxically such approaches infer a new form of
technological determinism, albeit one that predicts a future
that advantages women over men. The consequences of
this are explored in subsequent chapters. We shall see that

if the social relations of older technologies are presented in too rigid a form, then the new technologies come to be seen as too open and malleable. If the former give rise to an immobilizing pessimism, the latter obviate the need for feminist technopolitics. Recent studies of science and technology have transformed our understanding of the social relations of technologies, both old and new. What I suggest in this chapter is that the social shaping, or constructivist, perspective offers the possibility of a fruitful interchange with feminism that can overcome the unsatisfactory dualisms with which much feminist analysis has been plagued.

Beyond Technological Determinism

Although technological determinism has been a central theme in social theory (and re-emerges in recent debates on the network society, as well as in strands of feminist theory), it began to be seriously challenged as an intellectual position by the development, since the 1970s, of social studies of science and technology. Many of us who got involved then had a simple polemical purpose: to shake the stranglehold that a naïve 'technological determinism' had on the dominant understanding of the intertwining of society and technology. We were concerned that this view of technology, as an external, autonomous force exerting an influence on society, narrows the possibilities for democratic engagement with technology, by presenting a limited set of options: uncritical embracing of technological change, defensive adaptation to it, or simple rejection of it. Against this, the social studies of science and technology had its origins in a belief that the content and direction of technological innovation are amenable to sociological analysis and explanation, and to intervention.

Social scientists have increasingly recognized that technological change is itself shaped by the social circumstances within which it takes place. The new sociology of

technology set out to demonstrate that technological artefacts are socially shaped, not just in their usage, but especially with respect to their design and technical content.
Crucially, it rejected the notion that technology is simply
the product of rational technical imperatives; that a particular technology will triumph because it is intrinsically
the best. Technical reasons are vitally important. But we
need to ask why a particular technical reason was found
to be compelling, when it could have been challenged, and
what counts as technical superiority in specific circumstances. Studies show that the generation and implementation of new technologies involve many choices between
technical options. A range of social factors affect which of
the technical options are selected. These choices shape
technologies and, thereby, their social implications. In this
way, technology is a sociotechnical product, patterned by
the conditions of its creation and use.

There is now a vast literature and a variety of social
shaping approaches to the social study of technology.
Whereas references to the 'new sociology of technology'
were common in the 1980s, the terms 'constructivist
studies' or 'social studies of technology' (STS) are now
used to include actor-network theory, the social-construc-
tivist approach, social shaping and systems approaches to
technology studies.[1] As an introduction to the richness of
the field, it may be useful at this point to outline the principal concepts that inform it.

The idea of a technological 'system' or 'network' has
been key. Although technological innovation crucially
builds on previous technology, it does so not in the form
of separate, isolated devices but as part of a whole, as part
of a system. An automatic washing machine, say, can work
only if integrated into systems of electricity supply, water
supply and drainage. A missile, to take another example,
is itself part of an ordered system of component parts –
warhead, guidance, control, propulsion – and also part of
a wider system of launch equipment and command and
control networks. The need for a part to integrate into

the whole imposes major constraints on how that part is designed. A technological system is never merely technical: its real-world functioning has technical, economic, organizational, political and even cultural elements.

Take something you rarely think twice about – the electric refrigerator. We know from historians of technology that once upon a time you could choose between an electric refrigerator and a gas refrigerator, both equally effective.[2] General Electric had the financial resources to invest in the development of the electric model, while the manufacturers of gas refrigerators, although they had a product with real advantages from the consumer's point of view, lacked the resources to develop and market their machine. Economic power, not technical superiority, gave the electric refrigerator the edge over its competitor. However, the design of this kitchen 'white good' was also shaped by the post-Second World War spread of single-family houses, with correspondingly small-scale appliances. This built environment in turn sustains the cultural ideal of the separation of the public and private domestic spheres.[3] Gender roles and sexual divisions are part of the sociotechnical system or network.

This example illustrates the way technological decisions are the result of 'heterogeneous engineering': engineering 'social' as well as 'technical' phenomena by constructing an environment in which favoured projects can be seen as viable.[4] The usual economic explanation, which assumes that firms simply choose technologies that offer the maximum possible rate of profit, has also been the subject of much criticism. In response, some economists utilize the notions of technological trajectory, path dependence and lock-in to capture the mechanisms through which the evolution of a technology becomes more and more irreversible. The more that technologies are adopted and their problems resolved, the better their performance, and the greater their adoption. This clearly generates a powerful path-dependence over time, one that marginalizes competing or new technologies.

The social studies of technology emphasize that it is not necessarily technical efficiency, but rather the contingencies of sociotechnical circumstances and the play of institutional interests that favour one technology over another. Indeed, in situations of technical innovation, costs and profits are inherently uncertain; they cannot be taken as given facts. Economic calculations, such as estimating future costs and profits, are affected by the entire way a society is organized. Even markets are beginning to be understood as embedded in social networks.

The general point emerges most sharply when we consider the efficient use of labour, apparently a vital issue in technical change. David Noble's classic study of the development of automatically controlled machine tools in postwar USA shows how production technologies can reflect management's need for control over workers.[5] Noble notes that two options existed: 'record playback', whereby the machine merely replicated the manual operations of a skilled machinist, and 'numerical control', in which tool movements were controlled by a mathematical programme produced by a technician. He shows how the machine-tool suppliers, technologists and managers in the aerospace companies deliberately suppressed record playback in favour of numerical control, in order to reduce their reliance on the unionized craft-workers. As it happened, however, management found that it needed to retain skilled machinists to operate the new machines effectively. Thus the intentions underlying the technological design, to shift power from the shop-floor to the office, were not fully realized.

Furthermore, the linear model of innovation, which represents innovation as an activity restricted to engineers and computer scientists in research and development, producing finished products, has been questioned. Long after artefacts leave the industrial laboratory, the process of technological design is still taking place. Take the example of microwave ovens, a direct descendant of military radar technology, developed for food preparation in US navy submarines. When manufacturers first turned their eyes to the domestic market, they conceived of the microwave as a device to reheat prepared food for use by men, especially single men. As a result, it was marketed as a 'brown good', and sold next to hi-fi equipment, televisions and video recorders – goods for leisure and entertainment. This attempt to frame demand was unsuccessful, and subsequently both the product and the consumer were reconstituted, as a 'white good' for the housewife who still wants to cook.[6] The way in which women users appropriated this domestic technology was not foreseen by the male managers and engineers who designed it. The finished form of the microwave, which redefined the gendered character of the user, meant that the microwave literally shifted its place in the department store. It now sits alongside washing machines, fridges and freezers as a humdrum domestic appliance.

These cases highlight the divergent requirements and assumptions of technology developers and users. The making of the microwave is as much a story about the transformation of a quintessentially human activity, cooking, as it is about a technical invention. Technologies are not fixed at the innovation stage but evolve in their implementation and use. The idea of 'interpretative flexibility' captures this malleable character of technologies.[7] It emphasizes that there is nothing inevitable about the way technologies evolve. Rather, technological change is a contingent and heterogeneous process. Different groups of people involved with a technology can have very different understandings of that technology, including different understandings of its technical characteristics. Thus users can radically alter the meanings and deployment of technologies.

This point about the interpretative flexibility of technology refers not only to the symbolic meanings of technologies, but, importantly, also includes variation in criteria for judging whether a technology 'works'. Social studies of technology emphasize that machines work because they have been accepted by relevant social groups.

As a result, closure or stabilization occurs as some arte-facts become increasingly the dominant forms of the technology. The fact that a machine 'works' needs to be explained, rather than taken for granted.

This goes right to the heart of decisions about the vast technoscience research and development budgets in, for example, military weapons. Think for a moment about the crucial role that testing plays in attempts to justify the recent Bush Administration's missile defence shield. Yet, testing the accuracy of missiles has never been a straight-forward empirical matter. Donald MacKenzie's study of nuclear ballistic missiles reveals the extent to which de-finitions of accuracy and reliability are constructed rather than being simply factual.[8] For a start, the conditions for peacetime testing are fundamentally different from those under which missiles would need to operate during a war. MacKenzie's point, however, is both more profound and more general than this. He shows that testing inevitably involves a number of differently constructed background assumptions. As a result, no single test is ever accepted by all the parties involved as the ultimate arbiter. Indeed, those most closely involved in the scientific work of testing have a high degree of uncertainty about their knowledge of missile accuracy figures. The more one looks inside the 'black box' of nuclear weapons technology, or any other technological artefact, 'the more one realizes that "the technical" is no clear-cut and simple world of facts insu-lated from politics'.[9] Whether or not the 'Son of Star Wars' works will necessarily be as much a political as a techni-cal judgement.

Technology and society, then, are bound together inex-tricably, and the traffic between the two is reciprocal. Indeed, since the widespread adoption of 'actor-network theory', technology and society are no longer seen as separate spheres which influence each other.[10] Rather, the metaphor of a 'heterogeneous network' conveys the view that technology and society are mutually constitutive: both are made of the same stuff – networks linking human beings and non-human entities. The technological, rather than being a sphere separate from society, is part of what makes large-scale society possible. Their most controversial idea, that we cannot deny a priori that non-human actors or 'actants' can have agency, has helped us to understand the role of technology in producing social life.

The conception of the non-human as actant serves as a corrective to a rigid conception of social structure. It involves a view of society as a *doing* rather than a *being*. The construction of technologies is also a moving, relational process achieved in daily social interactions: entities achieve their form as a consequence of their relations with other entities.[11] This idea of the agency or power exercised by objects is generalized in Bruno Latour's concept of 'delegation to non-humans'.[12] His popular examples of automatic doors and road bumps show how technical objects define actors, the space in which they move, and the ways in which they behave and interact. Fittingly called 'sleeping policemen', road bumps are delegated the job of reducing motorists' speed where the rule of law does not suffice. In this way, it can be said that the material world itself exercises a kind of agency.

Studies of technoscience, then, have drawn attention to the neglect of technology or materiality in much social theory. Apart from research concerned with the impact of technology on society, the main focus of social science has been on social structure and social relations. Machines, artefacts and things have generally been treated as background context, rather than even-handedly alongside persons, institutions and events.[13] Technoscience approaches contribute to an understanding of social change by exploring how technologies and new forms of social life are co-produced. Material resources, artefacts and technology make society possible. To talk of 'social relations' as if they were independent of technology is therefore incorrect. Indeed, what we call 'the social' is bound together as much by the technical as by the social. Society itself is built along with objects and artefacts.

The common neglect of the power exercised by objects is not surprising given that when technical systems are completely integrated into the social fabric, they become 'naturalized', disappearing into the landscape. Take, for example, the way seemingly innocuous technologies such as photography and film assume, privilege and construct whiteness. Richard Dyer describes how it is extremely difficult to film black and white faces in the same film and do equal justice to both.[14] Each requires a completely different handling of lighting, make-up and film development. This means that when black and white actors are portrayed together, one group tends to lose out, and systematically it is black actors who are technologically shortchanged. Dyer traces this bias in the use of film techniques to the film industry's origins in the USA and Europe. From the mid-nineteenth century, experiments with the chemistry of photographic stock, aperture size, length of development and artificial light all proceeded on the assumption that what had to be got right was the look of the white face. By the time of film (some sixty years after the first photographs), technologies and practices were already well established, and shaped subsequent uses. So the very chemistry of photography represents a subtle form of technological apartheid.

From Gender-Blind to Gender-Aware

Within these mainstream – even malestream – bodies of work in technoscience, the ways in which technological objects may shape and be shaped by the operation of gender interests or identities have not been a central focus. This is as true of recent developments like actor-network theory as it is of earlier work. Whilst innovations are seen as sociotechnical networks, it has been largely incumbent on feminists studying technoscience to demonstrate that social relations include gender relations. So what is it about the social studies of technology that has made it hard for gender issues to be recognized? Several problems are involved, and I will outline them below.

To begin with, the marginalization of gender is indicative of a general problem with the mainstream methodology. This is related to the conception of power deployed by theorists in this genre. Using a conventional notion of technology, these writers have been concerned to identify and study the social groups or networks that actively seek to influence the form and direction of technological design. Their focus on observable conflict led to a common assumption that gender interests are not being mobilized. What many have overlooked is the fact that the exclusion of some groups, while not empirically discernible, may none the less impact upon the processes of technological development.

While the effects of structural exclusion on technological development are not easy to analyse, they should not be overlooked. Feminists have stressed that women's absence from spheres of influence is a key feature of gender power relations. Few women feature among the principal actors in technological design, as the sexual division of labour has excluded them from entering science, engineering and management. The problem with a primary focus on relevant social groups in the process of technological development is how to take account of those actors who are routinely marginalized or excluded from a network. Their absence is as telling as the presence of some other actors, and even a condition of that presence.

Within earlier socialist feminist approaches, it was relatively straightforward to discuss systematic male domination over women as a sex in terms parallel to those of class exploitation. Just as capitalists were deemed to have a relatively stable set of interests in maximizing profits, so men's interests as a sex were seen as institutionalized. The concept of patriarchy was often deployed as shorthand for institutionalized power relations between men and women, where gender is a property of institutions and historical processes, as well as of individuals. However, this was not meant to imply that men are a homogeneous group. For example, in

Feminism Confronts Technology I stressed that men's interests are not all identical, and that when it comes to influencing the design and development of a specific technology, some groups will have more power and more resources than others. So, long before the so-called postmodern challenge, 'difference' within the category of men, and between women, was already widely recognized.

By contrast, recent technology studies, such as actor-network theory, are more strongly influenced by a Foucauldian concept of power, where power is represented as capacity and effectiveness. Latour, for instance, suggests that power is not a possession – indeed, it must be treated as 'a consequence rather than a cause of action'.[15] Elsewhere Latour has argued that such constellations as classes, countries, kings or laboratories should not be treated as the cause of subsequent events, but rather as a set of effects.[16] In other words, they should be seen as consequences of sets of heterogeneous operations, strategies and concatenations. The job of the investigator, then, is not to discover final causes, but to unearth these schemes and expose their contingency.

In my view, an overemphasis on the enabling aspects of power can make it equally awkward to address the obduracy of the link between men and technology. Feminists' traditional concerns with women's access to technology, the differential impact of technology on women, and the patriarchal design of technologies have sat uneasily with this analysis of technology. The networks that actor-network theory is interested in are networks of observable interactions. While this theory perceives that artefacts embody the relations that went into their making, and that these relations prefigure relations implied in the use and non-use of artefacts, it is less alert to the inevitable gendering of this process. Such approaches do not always recognize that the stabilization and standardization of technological systems necessarily involve negating the experience of those who are not standard. Networks create not merely insiders, but also outsiders, the partially enrolled, and those who refuse to be enrolled. Attendance to practices of exclusion or avoidance and their effects are integral, not peripheral, to adequate descriptions of the process of network building.

A central argument of feminist theory has been that men are set up as the norm against which women are measured and found wanting. This involves celebrating certain forms of masculinity over any form of femininity. Indeed, this thesis is at the core of my book, *Managing Like a Man*, about the male definition of management.[17] An investigation of senior managers in multinational corporations, it shows how the hegemonic organizational culture incorporates a male standard which positions senior women managers as out of place. A parallel argument can be made that the standardization of networks implicitly places men's experiences and men's investments at the centre, without acknowledging their specificity. The corollary is the simultaneous denial of other realities, such as women's. So, while it is true that the imputation of social interests to social structures and institutions is always contestable and difficult to specify, there are nevertheless important contexts in which feminist analysis has no choice but to invoke interest explanations.

The absence of women from view is also a function of the concentration on issues of design. Innovation studies have underplayed the importance of enrolling other groups in the alliance of forces that enables a technological innovation to succeed. Agents in mainstream social studies of technology are most commonly male heroes, big projects and important organizations, in what Susan Leigh Star has described as a 'managerial or entrepreneurial' model of actor networks.[18]

A case in point is Bruno Latour's study of *Aramis*, a rapid transit system combining the efficiency of a subway with the flexibility of the car.[19] A professor of sociology and his engineering student investigate why an innovative technology, which would have transformed personal transport in Paris, failed. The story is told in multiple voices, including that of Aramis the artefact. As the intriguing plot unfolds, perspectives keep shifting to demonstrate that 'no technological project is technological first and foremost'. But neither does locating the project in its political, organizational or economic context render an adequate explanation. While networks of engineers, company executives, politicians and bureaucrats must be fully committed for the project to succeed, non-human resources also need to be enrolled. The relationship between humans and their technological creations can be understood only by seeing artefacts as fully involved in their own creation. This 'translation' model of innovation captures the diverse and multiple groups of individual people and things that jointly determine whether or not the project will be implemented.

Latour vividly illustrates how multiple networks continually transform the project as they become interested or disinterested. In the end, Aramis died when, like Frankenstein's monster, no one loved it any more. The story is not however as fully told as it purports to be. The voices we hear are those of male designers, politicians and technical experts, the male professor and his male student. Even the personification of Aramis as actant is implicitly a 'he'. Surprisingly, 'the love of technology', which serves as the subtitle of the book, is never examined as a peculiarly masculine feature of engineering culture. Men's love of machines embraces the car, which has a central place in hegemonic male culture. A fetishized object for many men, cars symbolize for them individual freedom, self-realization, sexual prowess and control.

Women's specific predisposition to cars is also overlooked. Many women value the car for its convenience in navigating their multiple roles. As mothers, unpaid domestic workers and paid workers, their journeys tend to be shorter, more complex and more multi-purpose than men's. They are more likely to travel with grocery bags, baby carriages and dependants. Women are also more vulnerable to sexual harassment and male violence when utilizing public transport, so the fact that Aramis consisted of separate, small cabins was a major flaw. Herein may lie important reasons for resistance to the innovation. The account of Aramis's network is incomplete because it does not include the gendered use of a transport system.

Once the lens is widened to include routine techno-science, manufacturing operatives, marketing and sales personnel, and the consumers and end-users of technologies, women immediately come into view. More women are literally present, the further downstream you go from the design process. Women are the hidden cheap labour force that produces routine science and technology; as the secretaries, cleaners and cooks, they are part of the sales force and the main users of domestic and reproductive technologies. The undervaluing of women's 'unskilled' and delegated work serves to make them invisible in main-stream technology studies. Actor-network theory is more interested in delegation to 'actants' than in the inequalities that arise in delegations among 'actors'.

Most scholars are habituated to considering gender issues only when their subjects are women. Mainstream studies have generally assumed that gender has little bearing on the development of technology because the masculinity of the actors involved was not made explicit. Despite a burgeoning literature on men and masculinities, the critical role played by technology in hegemonic mas-culinity has been largely ignored. It might be seen as ironic that the focus on agency has rarely sensitized these authors to issues of gendered subjectivity. By bracketing issues of sexual difference and inequality, mainstream technology studies fail to explore how technologies operate as a site for the production of gendered knowledge and knowledge of gender.

Combining Feminist and Technology Studies

Over the last decade, there has been an increasingly fruit-ful interchange between feminist and mainstream social studies of science and technology, although, as we have seen, this has not been symmetrical. The common ground is extensive, such as the constructivist emphasis on understanding technology as a sociotechnical product and the need to integrate the material, discursive and social elements of technoscientific practice. While feminists have drawn on many concepts from the social studies of technology, they have in turn modified them, partly in response to the problems outlined above. In the remainder of this chapter, I will briefly outline some of these attempts to reconfigure feminist and mainstream technology studies. Subsequent chapters will develop in more depth the issues foreshadowed here.

Technofeminist research has been at the forefront of moves to deconstruct the designer/user divide and, more generally, that between the production and consumption of artefacts. It is these divides that conventionally place men on one side and women on the other. One exemplary study that deliberately set out to combine an innovation study with a user study is that by Cynthia Cockburn and Susan Ormrod, who trace the trajectory of the microwave oven from its conception right through to its consumption.[20] Well aware that the standard technology studies' focus on invention underplays the role of women, the authors unravel the way that the sexual division of labour is mapped on to each stage in the journey of a domestic technology.

Like other domestic technologies, the microwave is designed by men in their capacity as engineers and managers, people remote from the domestic tasks involved, for use by women in their capacity as house-workers. Where women do enter the picture, apart from on the production line, is primarily as home economists, as their cooking expertise is crucial to the successful design of the artefact. These women see themselves as doing 'a kind of engineering or science', but it is not acknowledged as such by the predominantly male culture of engineers. Their technical skills are undervalued because of the strong association of cooking with femininity. As a result, even at the one point when women enter the innovation process, they wield little influence over the development of new technologies – evidenced, for example, by the lack of attention given to the browning of food in microwave cooking.

What is so original about the microwave study is that it follows the gendering processes through the various stages of the artefact's life. Gendering does not begin and end with design and manufacturing. Domestic technologies are also encoded with gendered meanings during their marketing, retailing and appropriation by users. Whilst the technology is made into a physical object during production, the symbolic meanings attaching to it are continually being negotiated and reinvented. Marketing and retailing play a key role in framing demand: 'there is an unclear dividing line between accurately *representing* the customer, *constructing* the customer and *controlling* the customer'.[21] In particular, the study explores the extent to which interpretative flexibility exists once a given commodity reaches the hands of the consumer. For purchasers, the consumption of a domestic commodity is an activity of self-expression, and a marker of gender identity. Thus marketing and consumption are all part of the social shaping of technology.

Thus the microwave study demonstrates how men's and women's different relationship to machines affects every stage in the life of a technology. As we saw earlier, even the microwave's colour reflects a gendered conception of household functions and, consequently, a gendered conception of potential purchasers – those concerned with domestic work as opposed to those concerned with leisure and entertainment. Whereas white goods are portrayed as serviceable and simple to use, brown goods are portrayed as complex, clever technologies that require skills in handling. This has much in common with recent studies about cultures of consumption that explore how consumers or users modify the meanings and values of technologies in the practices of everyday life.

However, culture is not just about the modification of goods in consumption, but also about how cultural meanings enter the production of goods. Cockburn and Ormrod conceive of technologies as in a continuous process of negotiation, as we 'domesticate' or make new technologies our own. However, this process is firmly located in the gendered assumptions of designers about prospective users. This technofeminist approach brings together the interpretative flexibility or malleability in how artefacts are read symbolically, with an understanding of how they are physically shaped and remade. It is therefore a study of a sociotechnical product that encompasses both material and immaterial networks.

Much of the best writing that combines feminist perspectives with the social studies of science and technology is in the area of biomedical innovations. In contrast to earlier feminist analyses of reproductive technology, this literature adopts a more nuanced version of the sociotechnical network that encompasses the medical profession, including the entry of women into the profession, as well as women's consumer power. Several recent studies on cervical cancer screening, for example, are concerned with the processes whereby technologies are deployed and appropriated by users.[22] They share with the microwave study the choice of a routine, mundane technology, as opposed to heroic technoscience. Eschewing the 'executive approach' that would necessarily focus on male technoscientists, they widen the lens to incorporate women 'downstream'.

One such study is concerned to show how a rather recalcitrant tool, the 'Pap smear', became the major cancer screening technology in the world. Monica Casper and Adele Clarke argue that several sets of concrete practices, or 'tinkering', have been used to make the Pap smear appear to be the right tool for the job. One such practice, often overlooked, has been the gendering of the division of labour in cytological screening. It appears that the success of the Pap smear depended on the feminization of the job of technician, with its accompanying low pay for difficult work. This makes clear the centrality of women's undervalued work in the standardization of a technology. The authors also explore the role of the women's health movement and public health activists, those outside the usual boundaries of the network, in successfully reshaping elements of the tool.

This approach combines actor-network theory with feminism and symbolic interaction. Clarke welcomes the emphasis on the role of non-human actors in scientific practice – that is, the pivotal role assigned to machines and natural objects in network building.[23] Such an approach helps to explain how particular scientific claims and technological innovations become successful – the requisite drawing together of discursive and material elements to enrol a large and diverse group of allies. However, Clarke sees her own 'social worlds analysis' as addressing the more common feminist critiques of mainstream technology studies, such as drawing attention to those who have been rendered invisible or disempowered by science in action. Her approach bridges internal and external concerns, locating scientific practice in the wider social and political context. Whereas most mainstream studies stop at the point where a technoscientific claim has developed enough power to start affecting people's lives, such feminist work draws attention to those effects and integrates them within their understanding of the sociotechnical.[24] The scientist or the executive is not given primacy. In this sense, it is very unlike the example of Aramis described above.

The technology of cervical screening is part of a long history of medical procedures designed for use exclusively on women's bodies. Indeed, medical technologies, such as sex hormones, have manufactured what we consider as our bodies. Nelly Oudshoorn's book *Beyond the Natural Body*, for example, shows how discourses about the natural body shaped the precise form of the contraceptive pill.[25]

Oudshoorn reminds us that the conceptualization of male and female bodies as essentially different, rather than similar, is a modern one, dating only from the eighteenth century. The identification of the female body as the Other resulted in positioning it as the quintessential medical object. Sex and reproduction were seen as the defining characteristics of women, and this was reflected in the establishment of gynaecology as a separate branch of medicine. With the rise of sex endocrinology in the 1920s and 1930s, the notion of the female body as the reproductive body was integrated into the hormonal model. Women's bodies thus became set apart as the prime site for biomedical practices of the body.

It was logical, then, for research on the first physiological contraceptive to be focused exclusively on women. Oudshoorn shows how discourses about the natural body shaped the Pill, and how the Pill, in turn, constructed women's bodies as universal with respect to their reproductive functions. The scientists who were developing the Pill attempted to design a universal 'one-size-fits-all' contraceptive technology, because they saw all women as being basically the same.

What is particularly interesting about this account is that it shows how these scientists succeeded in literally 'making' women the same. It turns out that the design of the Pill as a regime of medication, to be taken for twenty days a month, was shaped by moral considerations and notions of the natural body. Gregory Pincus, the American biologist who headed the research team, could have chosen any desired length for the menstrual cycle. He chose to make a pill that mimicked the 'normal' menstrual cycle. As a result, all Pill-users now have a regular cycle of four weeks, and the variety in menstrual cycles amongst women has been diminished. The Pill thus literally homogenized women's reproductive functions on a mass scale.

So far in this chapter, I have shown how 'older' technologies are malleable, and are constructed in ways similar

to those ascribed to new technologies. In addition, I have
shown how gender relations are crucial to that shaping
and have, in turn, been shaped within sociotechnical networks. I have chosen my examples of the microwave
cooker and biotechnologies deliberately, because they
show the continuities with domains claimed by recent
cyberfeminists to be radically different. The first shows
how cultures of consumption impinge upon technical
design, while the second is about the technical modification of bodies. To illustrate this further, I want to look at
the development of the typewriter. Once again, this is
important for drawing out the relation between old and
new technology: the typewriter keyboard remains the
primary interface for connection to cyberspace.

The strength of my final example is precisely that it, too,
locates women and machines in a historical context. Here
is a machine (the typewriter), an occupation (the typist)
and typing (a skill), all signified as feminine. A deterministic account sees the typewriter as having caused the feminization of office work, thereby rendering this gendering
entirely self-evident. However, the story is more complex,
as women, who were not meant to work, were to occupy
posts hitherto regarded as exclusively male. How, then, did
this dramatic gender inversion take place, and come to be
seen as the natural order of things?

The answer lies in two concurrent and interrelated
processes that were taking place as the typewriter was
introduced: the gendering of the typewriter as an object
and the construction of the practice of typing as feminine.[26] Indeed, in examining the early discourse about the
typewriter, it is difficult to separate descriptions of the
machine from those of its imagined and embodied users.
This makes it an ideal case study of the process by which
technology and a new social order between the sexes are
reciprocally shaped.

The typewriter was gendered right from its initial commercialization in the USA in the 1870s. The first models
happened to be produced in Remington's sewing-machine

workshops. This influenced their appearance and design, with the original models using a pedal to work the carriage return and mounted on a cast iron table like a sewing machine. The domestic nature of the technology was reinforced by its association with the piano-style keyboard. This affinity between the techniques of typing and playing the piano was drawn in many an analogy as making the machine suitable for young, educated, middle-class women, whose principal pastimes were playing the piano and embroidery. These associations, presented in a technological guise, lent credibility to the idea that the typewriter was a feminine tool.

At the same time, a number of discourses about a new femininity were emerging that promoted the idea that women could gain fresh ground by being employed in respectable jobs in business. This helped to construct the profession of typing as female. Emblematic of modernity, typists were presented as ushering in an era full of progress and promise. Observers and journalists regularly enthused about how well typing suited women, and how the typewriter was a woman's machine. These discourses permitted certain categories of women to enter the workforce, and sanctioned the intrusion of a female machine into the masculine world of the office. Although male stenographers were introduced to typing in the 1880s, as typing became more professionalized and more narrowly focused on technical skill and speed, the male figure of the stenographer gradually receded. It would be almost another hundred years before personal computers would make it natural once more for men to be seated at a keyboard typing, and for the practice of typing to lose its sex.

Conclusion

The way gender is theorized in these studies, which I would characterize as 'technofeminist', represents a major advance over previous work. In developing a theory of the gendered character of technology, there is inevitably a danger of adopting an essentialist position which sees technology as inherently patriarchal. Early feminist studies of gender and technology tended to theorize gender as a fixed, unitary phenomenon, which exists prior to and independently of technology, and then becomes embedded within it. The success of a technology was explained in terms of the economic or political interests of powerful groups, typically regarding these interests as established, and in need of no further explanation. Conversely, there is the danger of losing sight of the structure of gender relations through an overemphasis on the historical variability of the categories of 'technology' or 'women'.

The technofeminist studies discussed in this chapter have avoided both these dangers. They have not taken interests as static and pre-given, but they have also maintained the centrality of gender relations in the social shaping of technology. They have drawn upon developments in the social studies of science and technology, and have extended them within a feminist framework. In the process, they have given a more subtle and relational view of sociotechnical networks, and transformed our view of technologies, old and new.

This has parallels with wider developments in gender theory that have influenced cyber- and cyborg feminists such as Plant and Haraway, as we shall see in the next two chapters. Judith Butler, for example, has argued that men's and women's interests are not objectively given, but are collectively created.[27] Influenced by post-structuralism, she conceives of 'gender as a performance', in order to stress that gender is not fixed in advance of social interaction, but is constructed in interaction. Individuals act or perform gender, and demonstrate their gender identity. Gender is a social achievement that requires a constant process of reiteration.

This notion of performativity, or 'gender as doing', chimes with the actor-network theory view of society as a doing rather than a being (although, as we have seen, the

latter does not see that the 'doing' is always gendered and
that when women aren't there, men are still doing gender).
The construction of gender identities, like that of technologies, is a moving relational process achieved in daily
social interactions. The question is now posed in terms of
how interests are shaped together with the technology in
the making. This model of technological development
enables us to understand technologies and interests as
products of mutual alliances and dependencies among
groups involved in the specific technology. It follows from
this that gendered conceptions of users are fluid, and
subject to a variety of interpretations. The relationship
between particular gender power interests and their
inscription in technological innovation must be treated
with subtlety and its complexity recognized.

An emphasis on the contingency and heterogeneity of
technological change helps to locate its possibilities in
wider social networks. Such an analysis introduces space
for women's agency in transforming technologies. This is
not a space that has simply been opened up by new technologies. The feminist technoscience studies discussed in
this chapter have shown that it is also a characteristic of
existing sociotechnical networks, rather than simply a possibility presented by new technology in itself. However, it
is necessary to recognize not only possibilities, but also
constraints. Sociotechnical systems are not merely performed symbolically; they are also enacted materially. New
technologies are malleable, but they also reveal continuities of power and exclusion, albeit in new forms.

There is always a danger of confusing new developments in theory with new developments in the things that
theories are about. If performativity is a feature of all
social relations, and if technologies and new forms of gendered cultures are co-produced, then this has been the case
in the past, as much as it will be the case in the future. In
arguing that new technologies should be seen as having
continuities with older technologies, I am not arguing that
nothing has changed. We have new and better theories to

apply. There are revolutionary changes in technology under way. But the futures they encompass will require similar forms of analysis to those of existing technologies and a similar engagement with feminist technopolitics.

− 3 −

Virtual Gender

One individual can become a population explosion on
the Net: many sexes, many species.

Sadie Plant, *Zeros + Ones*

For the second half of the twentieth century, dreams of
freedom have been associated with space travel. Here was
the contemporary equivalent of man's historic quest to
conquer nature. Drawing on earlier Western colonial narratives about discovering the New Worlds, NASA named
its fleet of space shuttles after pioneering sea vessels:
Columbia, Discovery, Atlantis, Endeavour, Challenger.
These space explorations were imbued with the adventure
and romance of earlier maritime voyages. However, inter-
galactic travel was also about escaping earthly space and
time, and drew on the iconography of science fiction from
Star Trek to *Star Wars* to promote the utopian potential
of science. Defying gravity and floating weightless in space,
the body was in orbit. The image of the Earth as seen from
space has come to represent our greatest scientific achievement, that of sending a man to the Moon. And from the
perspective of space, Earth itself appears as a small vessel
carrying its human population of space travellers.

Today, space travel seems stalled. Astronauts and cosmonauts are modernist heroes in a narrative that was in part the product of Cold War competition between superpowers that no longer holds. Cyberspace, virtual reality and the Internet have taken over as the new frontiers for exploration and transcendence. They provide an opportunity on Earth to experience the romance of space, of seemingly infinite possibilities. Unlike real space travel, cyberspace is open to the many. While the dream of new communities in outer space remains remote, cyberspace has been quickly populated by disembodied settlers. Progress is still defined by technological enterprises, but it is digital rather than space technology that now excites the imagination with its more immediate and accessible possibilities. Rarely having made it into outer space, little wonder that feminists have seized upon new digital technologies for their potential to finally free women from the constraints of their sex.

The association of technology with ideals and hopes for the future has a long history. In *The Pearly Gates of Cyberspace*, Margaret Wertheim argues that cyberspace can be understood as an attempt to realize a technological version of the New Jerusalem.[1] The heavenly kingdom promises emancipation from frailties and failings of the body. Fantasies of transcending time and space and the limitations of mortal flesh abound. This idea of technology as the key to salvation has been a continuing theme in Western culture ever since the late Middle Ages; but now the notion of sacred salvation has been replaced with a secular version. Cyberspace has become the repository for immense religious yearning.

Our utopian communities are now to be found in the digital landscape, a non-hierarchical democratic space where global democracy can finally be realized. Spiritual desire has been mapped on to digitized space. The classic description of cyberspace in William Gibson's novel *Neuromancer* conjures up an almost biblical Heavenly City, an idealized *polis*.[2] The vision is one of immortality, transcendence and omniscience. 'Throughout Gibson's cyber-punk novels the body is disparaged as "meat", its prison-like nature contrasted with the limitless freedom that console cowboys enjoy in the infinite space of the matrix [that is, the Net].'[3] In this virtual world the tyranny of the flesh and of distance is overcome, as the old divisions of class, race, ethnicity, gender and sexuality are dissolved. This fiction infused expectations of the information super-highway as it became a reality, and encouraged people like Bill Gates to believe that it would be a powerful force for eliminating barriers of prejudice and inequality.

In this chapter, I shall discuss major feminist contribu-tions to our understanding and imagining of cyberspace and its possibilities. In particular, I shall look at how cyber-feminists have interpreted the new digital technologies and their networked character as potentially liberating for women. Before I do so, I want to set the scene with a brief discussion of recent arguments about the significance of the Internet and virtual communities.

Networked Community

Nowhere else is the lure of a blend of technology, networks and freedom so strong as in the widespread discussion of the virtual community and the idea that it represents a new form of sociability and social interaction. The currency of these ideas needs to be understood in the context of con-temporary debates about increasing social and personal fragmentation and the loss of civil society associated with late-modern societies.

The best-known American account of the consequences of declining social capital and the rise of individualization is Robert Putnam's *Bowling Alone*. Putnam argues that social inclusion depends upon societies with high social capital, characterized by dense social networks of recipro-cal social relations.[4] Citizens have retreated into the privacy of their homes, away from public spaces of face-to-face interaction, informal social activities and conviviality. For Putnam, this is linked with an earlier form of new communications technology – television. Its widespread penetration, together with generational change, has been the main cause of declining social capital. Television privatizes leisure time at the expense of sociability and civic engagement. Computer consoles and their privatized interactivity would seem to be a continuation of the trend that television first inaugurated.

The conviction that the Internet is the solution to social disintegration and individualism is no less popular than the idea that it will accelerate these trends. At both ends of the political spectrum, communication media are seen to play a key role – either as the cause of the problem or its cure. Indeed, cyber-gurus from Nicholas Negroponte to Manuel Castells proclaim that the Internet and cyberspace are bringing about a technological and social revolution.[5] Electronic networks are said to create new forms of sociability that will result in enhanced communities and greater world harmony.[6]

Castell's belief in the potential of enhanced Internet connectivity is reminiscent of McLuhan's argument in *The Gutenberg Galaxy* that television would be a restorer of organic culture and community in the global village.[7] In line with Howard Rheingold's original vision of *The Virtual Community*, cyberspace is portrayed as an informal public place where people can rebuild aspects of connectivity and community that have been lost in the modern world.[8] Virtual communities result from social collectivities that emerge from the Net to form webs of interpersonal ties in cyberspace.

The conservative overtones of these debates are apparent. They betray a nostalgia for an idealized past when people belonged to a harmonious community and spent time chatting with friends and neighbours. The destruction of community, and of most forms of communal solidarity, has been firmly signalled in sociological thought for a long while. At the same time, it has often been noted that the cosy, homogeneous, local community was a rare phenomenon. Tellingly, Rheingold's paradigmatic version of the virtual community reflects this nostalgia, with cyberspace providing for the restoration of the traditional community. The virtual community is the place where people can begin rebuilding aspects of community that have been lost, linked by commonality of interests and affinity rather than by accidents of physical proximity.

Castells, too, explicitly rejects the ideological opposition between the idealized community of the past and the alienated existence of the lonely Net citizen. For him, the Internet is the technological basis for a new form of society – the *Network Society*.[9] The Internet enables networks to substitute for spatial communities as major forms of sociability. This involves a redefinition of the concept of community as a network of interpersonal ties. Communities are based on social exchanges rather than physical location; the Internet enhances connectivity and social capital. This new pattern of sociability in the Network Society is characterized by networked individualism. 'Networked individualism is a social pattern, not a collection of isolated individuals. Rather, individuals build their networks, on-line and off-line, on the basis of their interests, values, affinities, and projects.'[10] The values of solidarity that are attributed to the traditional community can be realized without their conservative hierarchies.

The Internet is the central emblem of these changes: non-hierarchical, ungoverned, instant and value-based. The Internet creates a culture of 'real virtuality' which occurs in a 'space of flows and timeless time'. Real virtuality replaces stable, social foundations (place, nation, class or race) with virtual and changeable environments, which can exist in cyberspace quite separately from geographic locations or real cultural backgrounds. The virtual, networked space of flows is contrasted with the industrial-era 'space of places'. Networked individualism, organized around 'communities of choice', becomes the dominant form of sociability. For Castells, the aptly named *Internet Galaxy* marks a whole new epoch in the human experience.[11]

Although Castells is well aware that the Internet is open to abuse, his vision of the Internet is essentially positive. He describes Internet culture as made up of four layers: the techno-meritocratic culture, the hacker culture, the virtual communitarian culture, and the entrepreneurial culture. These features are all inscribed in the hacker culture that played a pivotal role in the construction of the Internet. This libertarian culture of computer programmers is based on the values of freedom: 'freedom to create, freedom to appropriate whatever knowledge is available, and freedom to redistribute this knowledge under any form and channel chosen by the hacker'.[12] Castells is clearly enamoured of the hacker community, a global virtual community based on creativity, co-operation, reciprocity, informality and a gift economy. The practice of these virtual communities epitomizes the practice of horizontal communication, a new form of global free speech on-line. Electronic networks are said to create new forms of sociability that will result in an enhanced 'global civil society' and greater world harmony.[13] For Castells, the culture of freedom is embodied in the Internet.

The problem with these theories of virtual community is ambiguity about the extent of their likeness to communities on the ground, and their relation to those grounded communities that necessarily remain. Like other virtual communitarians, their originators conflate virtual travel, communication and community. Spatial boundaries are still important, and residential communities potentially bring together a range of different groups of people. Indeed, inequalities reflected in residential areas have intensified, and it is not clear that virtual communities of choice will be any less homogeneous and mutually exclusive. In fact, writers are increasingly identifying a 'digital divide' in the access and use of the Internet.

The virtual community is a social vision that glosses over the fact that communities are also about material resources and power. This is an accepted feature of physical, proximate communities and, rather than being transformed by the Internet, conflicts are more likely to be carried into it. Significantly, theorists of virtual community emphasize 'communities of choice'; the freedom to choose associations and ties around the globe. Castells says that the 'Internet is produced by its use'. The hacker culture that he eulogizes is a male culture – in fact, a predominantly white middle-class culture, too. It is also a strange omission that he doesn't discuss the question of whose freedom is the issue. A major use of the Internet worldwide is for pornography, designed for a predominantly male audience and reflecting their choices. Moreover, cybersex entrepreneurs were the driving force behind key technical innovations, such as interactive CD-ROM software and improved on-screen image definition. Not only is there commercial pornography, but a parallel network of reciprocity and gift-giving of pornographic images. These, too, are communities of choice.

Furthermore, the central role of women in participating in and preserving communities is overlooked. Women have historically been the pre-eminent suppliers of emotional support in community networks and the major suppliers of domestic and unpaid community work. The 'culture of freedom' that Castells embraces seems to entail a freedom from responsibility for community networks and, therefore, to reflect an implicitly male perspective. Where women maintain family, friendship and neighbourhood ties, men have participated in a public sphere defined by instrumentalities of work. It was precisely this division that institutionalized men as designers of technology, and Castells does not address the gender relations of design. As we shall see, by taking up these lacunae, cyberfeminism provides a more comprehensive and powerful account than current social theories of digital technology.

Cyberfeminism: 'The clitoris is a direct line to the matrix'[14]

An optimistic – almost utopian – vision of the electronic community as foreshadowing the 'good society' is also characteristic of cyberfeminism. Although the above literature is silent on gender issues, it shares with some new strands of feminism the idea that Web-based technology generates a zone of unlimited freedom. For cyberfeminism, however, this means liberation for women. And just as cyber-gurus such as Castells have attracted many enthusiastic followers, so too have many feminists been drawn to writers such as Sadie Plant, the leading British exponent of cyberfeminism. Cyberfeminist discourse is particularly appealing to a new young generation, who have grown up with computers and pop culture in the 1990s, with their themes of 'grrrl power' and 'wired worlds'. In this section I want to read Plant's work as representative of this expanding trend within feminism.

In part, cyberfeminism needs to be understood as a reaction to the pessimism of the 1980s feminist approaches that stressed the inherently masculine nature of technoscience. In contrast, cyberfeminism emphasizes women's subjectivity and agency, and the pleasures immanent in digital technologies. They accept that industrial technology did indeed have a patriarchal character, but insist that new digital technologies are much more diffuse and open. Thus, cyberfeminism marks a new relationship between feminism and technology.

For Plant, technological innovations have been pivotal in the fundamental shift in power from men to women that occurred in Western cultures in the 1990s, the so-called genderquake. Old expectations, stereotypes, senses of identity and securities have been challenged as women gain unprecedented economic opportunities, technical skills and cultural powers. Automation has reduced the importance of muscular strength and hormonal energies and replaced them with demands for speed, intelligence and transferable, interpersonal and communication skills.[15] This has been accompanied by the feminization of the workforce, which now favours independence, flexibility and adaptability. While men are ill-prepared for a postmodern future, women are ideally suited to the new technoculture.

The digital revolution heralds the decline of the traditional hegemonic structures and power bases of male domination because it represents a new kind of technical system. For Plant, it is technology without *logos*. The standard way of thinking about technology is in terms of the application of reason in the domination and mastery of natural and social environments. Social hierarchies are put to work on nature in an orderly way to produce highly organized systems of social and technological power. For Plant, as for other feminist writers, this is fundamental to technology as a patriarchal system, and is bound up with masculine identities. This includes sexual identities. The 'ones' of Plant's title *Zeros and Ones* describe a singular male identity against which female identity is measured and found to be a nothing, a 'zero'. She cleverly uses the digital language of computers – sequences of zeros and ones – to evoke a new gendering of technology. There is a decided shift in the woman–machine relationship, because there is a shift in the nature of machines. Zeros now have a place, and they displace the phallic order of ones.

The Net, cyberspace, virtual reality and the matrix epitomize the shape of a new 'distributed nonlinear world'. They do not develop in predictable and orderly ways and cannot be subject to control. Innovations occur at different points in the Web and create effects that outrun their immediate origins. It is the ideal feminine medium where women should feel at home. This is because women excel within fluid systems and processes: their distinctive mode of being fits perfectly with the changes associated with information technology. The metaphors for this new technology are drawn from women's worlds, and looking back at the emergence of the new technology, Plant finds that women have been central to it. She traces a history of female superiority as programmers – or 'weavers of information' – from women's skills in weaving to their contributions to modern computing.

Plant derives from Freud the idea that weaving (just about the only technological initiative that Freud attributes to women) emerges as a simulation of pubic hair matted across the vagina. Plant reinterprets this idea that women are essentially suited to weaving by identifying weaving with the threads of communication that enmesh the world, the connections these allow, and the metaphor of the connectionist machines.

For Freud, matted hair hid women's lack, signifying their being other to men who defined the world. For Plant, the zero is the entrance to the matrix and a virtual world of infinite possibilities.

Plant sees continuity between the fluid identity of Luce Irigaray's women, Freud's hysterical women, and the anarchic, self-organizing qualities of the new machines. With the development of parallel processing, actions are distributed across a network of processors, instead of proceeding in series. The distinction is taken to be in tune with women's ability to work at several different things at the same time, while men are thought to be single-minded. Rather than the rigours of orthodox logic, the new technology favours distributed interaction and intuitive understanding which, Plant argues, were previously pathologized as hysteria. The fluidity of women's identity, previously regarded as reflecting a deprivation, becomes a positive advantage in a feminized future. Patriarchy's stereotyped account of women is inverted, and women's sexual difference is valorized.

Plant is aware that cybernetics also has military uses, but she does not believe these to be paramount. The new technology cannot be brought back under the old order. 'Cyberspace is out of man's control: virtual reality destroys his identity, digitalization is mapping his soul and, at the peak of his triumph, the culmination of his machinic erections, man confronts the system he built for his own protection and finds it is female and dangerous.'[16] Far from being a technology of male dominance, computing is a liberatory technology for women which delivers a post-patriarchal future.

Performing Gender in Cyberspace

In this section I will consider the cyberfeminist argument that new technologies involve not just the subversion of masculine identity, but a multiplicity of innovative subjectivities. Plant's metaphor of zeros and ones identifies the singularity of masculine identity against the multiplicity that, in the words of Irigaray, is inherent to the 'sex that is not one'. Digital technologies facilitate the blurring of boundaries between man and machine and male and female, enabling their users 'to choose their disguises and assume alternative identities'. For Plant, 'women, who know all about disguise, are already familiar with this trip'. Identity exploration challenges existing notions of subjectivity and subverts dominant masculine fantasies.

The idea that the Internet can transform conventional gender roles, altering the relationship between the body and the self via a machine, is a popular theme in recent postmodern feminism. The message is that young women in particular are colonizing cyberspace, where gender inequality, like gravity, is suspended. In cyberspace, all physical, bodily cues are removed from communication. As a result, our interactions are fundamentally different, because they are not subject to judgements based on sex, age, race, voice, accent or appearance, but are based only on textual exchanges. In *Life on the Screen*, Sherry Turkle enthuses about the potential for people 'to express multiple and often unexplored aspects of the self, to play with their identity and to try out new ones . . . the obese can be slender, the beautiful plain, the "nerdy" sophisticated'.[17] It is the increasingly interactive and creative nature of computing technology that now enables millions of people to live a significant segment of their lives in virtual reality. Moreover, it is in this computer-mediated world that people experience a new sense of self, which is decentred, multiple and fluid. In this respect, Turkle argues, the Internet is the material expression of the philosophy of postmodernism.

Interestingly, the gender of Internet users features mainly in Turkle's chapter about virtual sex. Cyberspace provides a risk-free environment where people can engage in the intimacy they both desire and fear. Turkle argues that people find it easier to establish relationships on-line and then pursue them off-line. Yet, for all the celebration of the interactive world of cyberspace, what emerges from her discussion is that people engaging in Internet relationships really want the full, embodied relationship. Like many other authors, Turkle argues that gender swapping, or virtual cross-dressing, encourages people to reflect on the social construction of gender, to acquire 'a new sense of gender as a continuum'.[18] However she does not reflect upon the possibility that gender differences in the constitution of sexual desire and pleasure influence the manner in which cybersex is used.

In a similar vein, Allucquére Rosanne Stone celebrates the myriad ways in which modern technology is challenging traditional notions of gender identity. Complex virtual identities rupture the cultural belief that there is a single self in a single body. Stone's discussion of phone and virtual sex, for example, describes how female sex workers disguise crucial aspects of identity and can play at reinventing themselves. She takes seriously the notion that virtual people or selves can exist in cyberspace, with no necessary link to a physical body. As an illustration of this, Stone recounts the narrative about the cross-dressing psychiatrist that has become an apocryphal cyberfeminist tale. Like many stories that become legends, it is a pastiche of fiction and fact, assembled from diverse sources, including real events.[19]

It is the story of a middle-aged male psychiatrist called Lewin who becomes an active member of a CompuServe chat line, a virtual place where many people can interact simultaneously in real time. One day Lewin found he was conversing with a woman who assumed he was a female psychiatrist. Lewin was stunned by the power and intimacy of the conversation. He found that the woman was more open to him than were his female patients and friends in real life. Lewin wanted more, and soon began regularly logging on as Julie Graham, a severely handicapped and disfigured New York resident. Julie said it was her embarrassment about her disfigurement that made her prefer not to meet her cyberfriends in person.

Over time, Julie successfully projected her personality and had a flourishing social life on the Internet, giving advice to the many women who confided in her. Lewin acquired a devoted following and came to believe that it was as Julie that he could best help these women. His on-line female friends told Julie how central she had become to their lives. Indeed, the elaborate details of Julie's life gave hope particularly to other disabled women as her professional life flourished and, despite her handicaps, she became flamboyantly sexual, encouraging many of her friends to engage in Net sex with her. Her career took her around the world on the conference circuit, and she ended up marrying a young police officer.

Julie's story is generally taken to show that the subject and the body are no longer inseparable; that cyberspace provides us with novel free choices in selecting a gender identity irrespective of our material body. Stone argues that by the time he was exposed, Lewin's responses had ceased to be a masquerade, that he was in the process of *becoming* Julie. However, this story can be read in a radically different manner, one that questions the extent to which the cyborg subject can escape the biological body.

Although Julie's electronic manifestation appears at first sight to subvert gender distinctions, it can be just as forcefully argued that it ultimately reinforced and reproduced these differences. For the women seeking Julie's advice, her gender was crucial. They wanted to know that there was a woman behind the name; this is what prompted their intimacies. Julie's gender guided their behaviour and their mode of expression. 'It rendered her existence, no matter how intangible and "unreal" Julie appeared at first, extremely physical and genuine.'[20] When Julie was unmasked as a cross-dressing man years later, many women who had sought her advice felt deeply betrayed and violated.

It was the 'real' disabled women on-line who first had suspicions about the false identity, indicating that there are limits on creating sustainable new identities in cyberspace. Relationships on the Internet are not as free of corporeality as Stone, Turkle and Plant suggest. Although computer-mediated communication alters the nature of interaction by removing bodily cues, this is not the same as creating new identities. Just because all you see is words, it does not mean that becoming a different person requires only different words, or that this is a simple matter. Choosing words for a different identity is problematic.[21] The choice of words is the result of a process of socialization associated with a particular identity. It is therefore very difficult to learn a new identity without being socialized into that role. Although mimicry is possible, it is limited, and is not the same as creating a viable new identity.

Research on artificial intelligence and information systems now emphasize the importance of the body in human cognition and behaviour. Moreover, the sociology of scientific knowledge has taught us that much scientific knowledge is tacit (things people know but cannot explain or specify in formal rules) and cannot be learned explicitly. So it is with becoming a man or a woman. Lewin's false identity was discovered by people who had been socialized in the role that Lewin adopted: namely, that of a disabled woman. Bodies play an important part in what it means to be human and gendered.

That this narrative is about a man posing as a woman is not merely incidental as there is evidence that many more men adopt a female persona than vice versa. The masculine discursive style of much communication on the Web is well recognized. 'Flaming' or aggressive on-line behaviour, including sexual harassment, is rife, and has a long lineage all the way back to the original hackers who developed the first networked games such as the notorious Dungeons and Dragons/MUD games. These games were designed by young men for the enjoyment of their peers. This reflected the computer science and engineering 'nerd' technoculture that produced the Internet and excluded women from participation.

Cyberspace first appeared as 'a disembodied zone wilder than the wildest West, racier than the space race, sexier than sex, even better than walking on the moon' in cyberpunk fiction.[22] It promised to finally rupture the boundaries between hallucination and reality, the organic and the electronic. For cyberpunks, technology is inside the body and the mind itself. Textual and visual representations of gendered bodies and erotic desire, however, proved less imaginative. It was new technology with the same old narratives. Here was a phallocentric fantasy of cyberspace travel infused with clichéd images of adolescent male sex, with console cowboys jacking into cyberspace.

A fan of cyberpunk, Plant's project is to feminize this terrain. Rather than casting women as passive victims or sex objects, she maintains that the new interactive multimedia radically recode pornographic consciousness and culture. As an arena where polymorphous sexualities can be performed, cyberspace undermines binary heteronormative subjectivities. Even sado-masochistic iconography can be reappropriated by technologically savvy cyberfeminists.

A popular, contemporary version of these adventure games does feature a female character – notably Lara

Croft, in the popular Tomb Raider game, alternatively seen as a fetish object of Barbie proportions created by and for the male gaze or as a female cyberstar. The orthodox feminist view of Lara Croft sees her as a pornographic techno-puppet, an eternally young female automaton. By contrast, postmodern gender and queer theorists stress the diverse and subversive readings that Lara Croft is open to.[23] For some she is a tough, capable, sexy adventurous female heroine. For others, Lara as drag queen enables men to experiment with 'wearing' a feminine identity, echoing the phenomenon of gender crossing in Internet chat rooms.

While Lara may offer young women an exciting way into the male domain of computer games, much of the desire projected on to this avatar is prosaic. The game even features a Nude Raider patch that removes Lara's clothing. To cast her as a feminist heroine is therefore a long bow to draw. Perhaps we should let her creator Toby Gard have the last word: 'Lara was designed to be a tough, self-reliant, intelligent woman. She confounds all the sexist clichés apart from the fact that she's got an unbelievable figure. Strong, independent women are the perfect fantasy girls – the untouchable is always the most desirable.'[24]

Technology as Freedom

Much of the pessimistic critical literature on science and technology has seen technology in a deterministic way, as potentially dehumanizing and running out of control. Plant offers a twist on this theme. She *celebrates* cybertechnology out of control because, for her, out of control signifies freedom from male control. The metaphors by which she builds her case are, however, weakly related to the social reality of new technology relations, and the instances she cites are misconstrued. For example, her history of women's involvement in technological developments, such as the typing pool and the telephone exchange, are in fact examples of women's subordination. She gestures towards recognition that the interconnectivity of the Internet is a product of global capitalism that enables new forms of production and exploitation. Yet her apparent awareness of women's exploitation does not stop her from seeing such technology as necessarily empowering women.

A more consistent version of this position would be that technology itself is plastic, and therefore the same technology can have contradictory effects, as the social relations and context of their use are all important. But Plant does not follow this path. Instead, she claims that women's affinity with digitalization means that it is inherently freeing. For Plant, there is a direct causal relationship between communication technologies and the particular cultural forms they come to be associated with. Her homage to the Internet closely echoes Marshall McLuhan's famous aphorism, 'The medium is the message', and she acknowledges his legacy.[25] Like McLuhan, she fails to distinguish between technical inventions (the digitalization of data), the socially instituted technology (the Internet), and its attendant cultural forms (e-mail, web sites, interactive multimedia, etc.).[26] As a result, the crucial influence of media corporations and communications institutions, within which technologies develop and which circumscribe their use, is ignored.

Plant's abstract theory of the Internet thus reproduces McLuhan's technological determinism, and can be criticized in precisely the terms that Raymond Williams applied to McLuhan in *Television: Technology and Cultural Form*.

> It is an apparently sophisticated technological determinism which has the significant effect of indicating a social and cultural determinism: a determinism, that is to say, which ratifies the society and culture we now have, and especially its most powerful internal directions. For if the medium – whether print or television – is the cause, all other causes, all that men [*sic*] ordinarily see as history, are at once reduced to effects. Similarly, what are elsewhere seen as effects, and as such subject to social, cultural, psychologi-

cal and moral questioning, are excluded as irrelevant by comparison with the direct physiological and therefore 'psychic' effects of the media as such.[27]

As Williams so forcefully points out in relation to McLuhan, the political consequence of this avant-gardist celebration of the 'new media' is paradoxically to legitimate the existing social order. Plant is similarly exposed as politically conservative. If digital technology is inherently feminine, whoever controls or uses it, then no political action is necessary. Cyberfeminism may appear to be anarchist and anti-establishment, but, in effect, it requires for its performances all the latest free-market American capitalist gizmos.

Plant's utopian version of the relationship between gender and technology is perversely post-feminist. Rather than wanting to erase gender difference, Plant positively affirms women's radical sexual difference, their feminine qualities. It is a version of radical or cultural feminism dressed up as cyberfeminism and is similarly essentialist. The belief in some inner essence of womanhood as an ahistorical category lies at the very heart of traditional and conservative conceptions of womanhood. What is curious is that Plant holds on to this fixed, unitary version of what it is to be female while, at the same time, arguing that the self is decentred and dispersed. Her *mélange* of postmodern/French feminist/psychoanalytic theories of the fractured identities of woman, with sets of embodiments, might have led her to emphasize the differences between, as well as within, individuals. However, she does not connect these theories on multiple identities and bodies with the multiple lived experiences that give rise to them. Rather, throughout Plant's analysis there is dissonance between her appeal to universal feminine attributes and her conceptualization of women's fragmented identities.

Like much of the literature on cyberculture, Plant does not consider in any depth women's actual experience of computer facilities. Her depiction of the Internet bears little relation to how most women use it. Internet usage is predominantly for instrumental e-mail, related to work functions. The web sites most visited by women in the USA are in fact shopping and health sites, such as pampers.com, avon.com and oilofolay.com. Furthermore, Plant overlooks the physical environments within which women's access to the Internet takes place. For example, the Internet Cafe is often seen as exemplary of a gender-neutral public space. Yet emerging field-work on cyber-cafes confounds this picture. While new gender alliances are being forged through interactions between computers, staff and customers at cafes, old stereotypes of gender and technology are also in evidence. Most obviously, women's bodies are used to encapsulate the cyber-vibe of the cafe, as in the recurring sculpture of glossy red lips clamped around a computer disc. Observers of Internet use conclude that specific local cultures of place and space, including the 'offline landscapes' of cyber-cafes, are decisive in interpreting the feminist potential of the Net.[28]

For most women, however, their main encounter with computers is in the workplace. Computing remains a very male industry, with women having limited career prospects in the information technology, electronics and communications sectors. More broadly, the shift to the information or knowledge economy has been marked by an enormous growth of contingent workers, with women making up the majority of part-time and temporary workers. This increase in flexible work could not have occurred without the proliferation of the information and communications technologies that support it. Changes to work organization as a result of computerization have been mixed. As well as enhancing opportunities for autonomy and control, many working women identify the move from typewriters to computers, for example, with the intensification and monitoring of work. The dramatic growth in economic inequality between women with very different qualifications, skills and labour market resources makes it impossible to generalize about women's experiences with computers. The 'feminization of work' that Plant lauds is characterized as much by a proliferation of casual, low-paid jobs as by high-flying, globally wired women. New technologies may be 'epistemologically open', but many of their current forms are similar in their material relations to pre-existing technologies.

Conclusion

Cyberfeminists are excited by the possibilities that the Web offers to women. They have moderated the tendency in second-wave feminism to portray women as victims by stressing their agency and capacity for empowerment. Young women in particular are orienting and experiencing themselves in relation to new media technologies, differently from previous generations. New communication technologies have certainly brought about new techniques for sociality and new ways of gender bending. While there is a thrilling quality to these pioneering endeavours, we must not be hypnotized by the hype that is now ubiquitous. There is a risk that the focus on cyberspace as the site of innovative subjectivities that challenge existing categories of gender identity may exaggerate its significance.

Throughout cyberfeminist thought, there is a tension between the utopian and the descriptive. The utopian imagining is attractive and can provide a critical perspective on existing social relationships. This is especially valuable in the current political climate, where neo-liberal ideologies predominate after the end of the Cold War. However, the force of utopian thinking derives precisely from being about a place that does not exist, in the light of which the present can be criticized. Utopia is about *nowhere*, not *now-here*. By conflating this distinction, cyberfeminism presents the utopian imagining of cyberspace as a more or less adequate description of aspects of what currently exists.

If what is imagined is in the process of becoming, there is no need for politics to bring it into being. In this way, cyberfeminism is post-feminist. Technology itself replaces the need for programmes of social and political change. The very value of utopian thinking is undermined. Its value is precisely to create a space between contemporary experience and political desires, and to turn them optimistically towards the construction of new forms of politics. This has always been the project of feminism, and was one of the reasons for its hostility towards deterministic social theories. The underlying critique holds good even when what is determined is said to be in the interests of women. It would be unwise to presume that the direction of technological change has simply changed sides to benefit women where once it benefited men.

The uncritical implications of the conflation of the utopian and the descriptive are more straightforward in the arguments of writers like Castells and Rheingold discussed at the start of the chapter. The virtual networks that embody freedom and represent 'communities of choice' are described in terms that are reminiscent of neo-liberal values of individual choice and voluntary association. The disembodied character of these values has been the subject of powerful feminist criticism over the last decades. It is not just that technology is seen as an alternative to politics. On closer examination, the values which these writers embrace are themselves bound up with much that feminists have criticized.

Utopian thinking is indispensable to feminist politics, but it needs a clearer distinction between description and imagination to play a useful role. Plant's strength is her deployment of metaphors to transform the way we think about the woman–machine relationship. However, even as metaphors, they are somewhat strained. The fluidity and mobility of the nomadic subject exploring the Net utilizes the metaphor of exploration and travel, suggesting that it is close to female experience. The narrative of a journey is central to much utopian thought, yet it is much more an expression of masculinity. Noting the proliferation of vocabularies of travel in cultural criticism, Janet Wolff argues that just as there are real disparities in women's access to and modes of travel, so the use of metaphors of travel necessarily produces androcentric tendencies in theory.[29] Western masculine narratives traditionally view travel as an escape from feminine domesticity, the site of stasis and containment. While men take to the road or the information superhighway to find themselves, and social theorists embrace mobilities, circulating networks, and liquid modernity as their central concerns, women keep the home fires burning as they did in the physically proximate communities that virtual networks are held to have replaced.[30]

Romanticized ideas of virtual voyages similarly echo the gendered division of human activity in which the male life of the mind is valued over women's confinement to the visceral body. As feminists have long pointed out, the embodied and situated nature of knowledge has been denied precisely because it is based upon the invisible work of women. Rather than dreaming of a flight from the body, feminism has argued for men to be fully embodied and take their share of emotional, caring and domestic work. To express this in computer jargon, an emancipatory politics of technology requires more than hardware and software; it needs wetware – bodies, fluids, human agency.

– 4 –

The Cyborg Solution

I want the readers to find an 'elsewhere' from which to
envision a different and less hostile order of relationships among people, animals, technologies, and land
... I also want to set new terms for the traffic between
what we have come to know historically as nature and
culture.

Donna Haraway, *Primate Visions*

Nowhere is the relationship between gender and technology more vigorously contested than in the sphere of
human biological reproduction. Women are the bearers,
and in most societies the primary nurturers, of children.
This means that reproductive technologies are of particular significance to them. Birth control has been a major
issue for all movements for women's equality, and much
feminist scholarship has been devoted to uncovering
women's struggle throughout history against the appropriation of medical knowledge and practice by men.

Central to this analysis, and of increasing relevance
today, is the perception that the processes of pregnancy
and childbirth are directed and controlled by ever more
sophisticated and intrusive technologies. The rapid
advance of genetic technologies and the possibility of

human cloning have created a prospect of life itself becoming another commodity. As embryo screening tests become more sophisticated, cheaper and more widely available, parents are faced with increasing social and moral pressures to utilize the information available to ensure that their offspring are healthy and free of genetically linked disorders. Advances in biotechnology offer the possibility of selecting babies for whom certain 'genetic advantages' can be assured – for example, in aspects of physical appearance, intelligence or personality traits.

Feminists were among the first to make the links between reproductive technologies, genetic engineering and eugenics. As we have seen, the focus of much of the early analysis by radical feminists was a determination to reclaim motherhood as the foundation of women's identity. Implicit in this view is a concept of reproduction as a natural process, inherent in women alone, and a theory of technology as patriarchal, enabling the male exploitation of women and nature. Motherhood was seen as both embodied and natural, a biological fact of nature, into which technologies might intervene, but still reducible to the biological and the natural. Like ecological feminists, radical feminists celebrated the identification of women with nature and saw women as having a special responsibility to ensure the integrity of human and natural life on earth.

It is not surprising, then, that efforts to mobilize a feminist or environmental politics of technology often take the form of resistance to technological development. This can be seen in the way the Green movement has expanded its range of concerns to include the preservation not only of forests, fish and animals but also of peoples. Having found that indigenous communities often get in the way of preserving the pristine natural environment, a recent article in *Scientific American* (May 2002) advocates a new biodiversity conservation strategy. This would involve conservationists outbidding logging companies and paying local landowners to preserve the forest, and thus keep themselves in their original state. Although a long way from the age of innocence, such a politics is driven by the desire to return to the Garden of Eden, and preserve the last vestiges of untainted nature.

The resurgence of scientific interest in genetic explanations for a variety of human behaviours and personality traits lends increased legitimacy to a new kind of genetic determinism. Social problems as diverse as school failure, alcoholism, delinquency and even homosexuality are increasingly attributed to our genetic make-up. This is exemplified in the academic fields of evolutionary psychology and behavioural genetics, which seek to explain a wide range of human characteristics in terms of their evolutionary survival and adaptation value to the species. Where feminists have argued that gender roles are socially constructed and open to reconstruction, this new argument suggests that gender roles are hard-wired in the genes. The notion that the script of our lives is largely written in our genes has taken root in the popular imagination.

Embracing Science and Technology

Leading the charge against those who reject technology in favour of a return to a mythical natural state and against the proponents of a genetic determinism, Donna Haraway has become the most influential feminist commentator on technoscience. This chapter is therefore devoted to an examination of her contribution and the myriad ways in which her work has been pursued and popularized. Haraway urges us to engage fully with the dramatic challenges generated by our informational technocultural times. She embraces the positive potential of science and technology, to create new meanings and new entities, to make new worlds. While there is much in those spheres she would wish to see change, she eschews an 'eco-feminist' celebration of women's spiritual closeness to an unpolluted nature. She regards the language of pollution as politically dangerous, too close to that of the eugenic cleansing promoted in scientific racism and colonialist discourses. Famously, and provocatively, she prefers to be an impure 'cyborg' – a cybernetic organism, such as an animal with a human-made implant – rather than a pure, eco-feminist 'goddess'.

Haraway's optimism is a refreshing antidote to the technophobia that characterizes much radical feminist and ecological thought. Indeed, in stressing the liberatory potential of science and technology, she is rephrasing an old modernist theme linking science with progress. While critical of many aspects of the way this happens, such as extending private property to include life forms (patenting), she warns against a purist rejection of the 'unnatural', hybrid entities produced by biotechnology. Sharing her 'frank pleasure' at the introduction into tomatoes of a gene from flounders, which live in cold seas, which enables tomatoes to produce a protein that slows freezing, she revels in the very difficulty of predicting what technology's effects will be.[1] The 'lively, unfixed, and unfixing' practices of science and technology produce 'surprises [that] just might be good ones'.[2] Haraway's ground-breaking work has transformed feminist scholarship on technoscience.

Let me begin by briefly considering 'A manifesto for cyborgs: science, technology, and socialist feminism in the 1980s'. This essay originally appeared in the American journal *Socialist Review*, in 1985, and soon achieved a cult-like status among academic feminists. The debate about the micro electronic revolution was raging, and the socialist feminist orthodoxy was laden with gloomy predictions about what the future held for women. The computerization of work would lead to widespread deskilling of workers, health hazards and massive unemployment. Developments in *in vitro* fertilization, egg donation and surrogacy were seen to fuel a conservative family politics.

Feminist historians and philosophers of science were emphasizing that Western scientific knowledge was inherently patriarchal. The efforts of liberal feminists to improve women's access to science and engineering were showing few signs of success. There seemed little cause for optimism in the wider world of international politics. The Reagan era in the USA and Thatcherism in the UK were demolishing the welfare state and attacking the labour movement. The experiment with communism would soon be over, as the Soviet Union was brought to its knees. The victory of Western capitalism was complete. Socialists and feminists seemed to be caught in unfulfilled dreams of the past.

Against this background, Haraway's upbeat and visionary manifesto for cyborgs, pointing to a bright future for socialist-feminism in the new technological age, was rapturously received. While the essay is firmly based on the radical critique of science as the product of capitalism, militarism, colonialism, racism and, crucially, male domination, it sees cybertechnology as a potential asset for emancipation. It is precisely this conception of science as a social process, a material-semiotic practice, that gives her hope. If science and technology are not outside society, but are an integral part of it, then 'taking responsibility for the social relations of science and technology means refusing an anti-science metaphysics, a demonology of technology, and so means embracing the skilful task of reconstructing the boundaries of daily life, in partial connections with others, in communication with all our parts'.[3]

For Haraway, then, informatics, communications and biotechnologies provide fresh sources of power for women world-wide, which in turn require new ways of doing feminist politics. Her adoption of the optimistic register was prescient, as the 1990s dot.com boom would see the stock market rashly invest billions of dollars in a putative 'new economy'. Based in Santa Cruz, close to Silicon Valley, Haraway was perhaps well placed to feel the pulse of change.

From Man of Science to FemaleMan©

Largely due to the excitement generated by her cyborg trope, Haraway has played an important role in bringing the insights of science studies to a much wider audience. Building on scholarly traditions in the history, philosophy and sociology of science, Haraway foregrounds the constitutive role of metaphor, analogy, classification, narrative and genealogy in the production of scientific or natural facts. Trained in developmental biology and the history of science, Haraway in her work on primatology – the systematic study of apes and monkeys – radically redefined the science–culture matrix. In *Primate Visions: Gender, Race and Nature in the World of Modern Science* she argues that primatology works as a political order involving the negotiation and renegotiation of boundaries.[4] This occurs through ordering differences: those of science and ideology, nature and culture, male and female. For Haraway, science is culture in an unprecedented sense. Her central concern is to expose the 'god trick', the dominant view of science as a rational, universal, objective, non-tropic system of knowledge: 'the detached eye of objective science is an ideological fiction, and a powerful one'.[5] Science is not disembodied truth; it is social knowledge, a form of life and a material-semiotic practice utilizing narrative forms similar to those of other social knowledges.

This argument is further developed from the standpoint of the 'modest witness' to the scientific revolution that Haraway adopts as the title of *Modest_Witness@Second_Millennium.FemaleMan©_Meets_Oncomouse*[TM]. The modest witness figure is borrowed from an engaging historical study of the experimental way of life at the centre of modern science (by Steven Shapin and Simon Schaffer).[6] It examines the role of the scientific community in establishing the practice we now know as science. The topic is the controversy that took place in the 1660s and early 1670s between Thomas Hobbes and Robert Boyle over Boyle's experiments with the air pump, a device designed to create a vacuum by removing air from a glass globe. It aimed to provide a model of how authentic scientific knowledge could be secured, and it became in effect an emblem of the new experimental science. Ultimately Boyle's view prevailed, and Shapin and Schaffer demonstrate that not one, but three, technologies were crucial to the establishment of the practice of experimental science. In addition to the material technology of the air pump, there was a 'literary technology', whereby the phenomena produced by the pump were conveyed to those who were not direct witnesses, and a 'social technology', incorporating the conventions which experimental philosophers should use in dealing with each other and considering knowledge-claims.

It was these social and literary technologies of proper witnessing that allowed the air pump to establish objective matters of fact, independent of religion and politics. The experiment had to be witnessed by a special community in public space, so as not to be thought of as an activity for secret societies, but as something 'true' that 'anyone' could see. In seventeenth-century England, this meant face-to-face, gentlemanly standards for assessing truth telling. The ideal witness to scientific experimentation was primarily *modest* – that is, an uninvolved, neutral and patient observer. The laboratory was open, but only to those who could observe experiments without emotion and report what they had seen with honesty. 'Matter of fact' is 'both an epistemological and a social category' – 'an artifact of communication and whatever social forms were deemed necessary to sustain and enhance communication'.[7] Modern scientific knowledge, with its core concepts of scientific rationality, objective truth and logical positivism, was from the outset a fundamentally social practice. As Haraway observes, from these modest witnesses arises an immodest narrative, a grand narrative of scientific reason.

Haraway's modest witness endorses Shapin and Schaffer's perspective while reinterpreting this classic science studies narrative in a subversive way. S/he observes that the invisible witness to the experimental life was and is actually a white European male. Only members of the Royal Society or their guests could observe the workings of Boyle's air pump. Women were literally excluded, having to wait until 1945 to be admitted to the Royal Society in London, almost 300 years after Boyle's first experiments. Even today, women comprise less than 4 per cent of the Society's membership, prompting accusations that it remains a club for white, elderly men. Haraway's point, however, is more profound than this. She argues that gender and race, by their very absence, are at the heart of how modern scientific knowledge was conceived. Mainstream science studies have been blind to the way science was materialized as a taken-for-granted male practice.

Here Haraway is drawing on a rich literature on gender and science, dating from the early 1980s.[8] Feminist scholars re-examined the Scientific Revolution, arguing that the science which emerged was based on the masculine ideology of mastering and exploiting the Earth, which in turn relied on the use of gendered imagery to conceptualize nature. The rape and torture metaphors in the writings of Francis Bacon and the other fathers of modern science illustrate this point.[9] During the fifteenth to seventeenth centuries in Europe, both nature and scientific inquiry were conceptualized in ways modelled on men's violent and misogynous relationships to women, and this modelling contributed to the distinctive gender symbolism of the subsequent scientific world-view. Central to the formation of modern Western science was the cultural association of nature with passive, objectified femininity and of culture with active, objectifying masculinity. Culture versus nature, mind versus body, reason versus emotion, objectivity versus subjectivity, the public realm versus the private realm – in each dichotomy the former must dominate the latter, and the latter in each case is systematically associated with the feminine. These dualistic gender metaphors were the foundation of purportedly value-neutral scientific thought.

Haraway challenges these dualisms through the metaphor of FemaleMan©, which she derives from the science fiction writer Joanna Russ. FemaleMan© promises a new way of engaging in and with science. Whereas the man of science has a strong, bounded sense of self which is projected as universal and culture-free, FemaleMan© brings into science the hybrid and messy identities that the male narrative of scientific objectivity sought to purify.

Again it is important to note that Haraway is not anti-science. Her understanding of the ways in which sex and gender are themselves defined and constituted in the life sciences makes her want to build a stronger science. She is sympathetic to feminist attempts to develop a successor science based on 'standpoint theory' – that is, feminist epistemologies which privilege women's 'ways of knowing' above others.[10] The key idea here is that knowledge produced from women's standpoint or experience is distinctive in form as well as in content, and should be the foundation of a more comprehensive, truer science. Haraway's proposition is the notion of 'situated knowledges', which avoids any essentialist idea of a universal women's perspective. Instead, she calls for a feminist science that acknowledges its own contingent, located foundations just as it recognizes the contingent, located foundations of other claims for knowledge.

In common with other feminist critics of science, then, Haraway opposes the orthodox version of science as uncommitted and context-free, viewing multiplicity as offering a 'stronger objectivity' than that of the man of science based upon his singular identity. Haraway's postmodern construction of FemaleMan© however makes her extremely sceptical of grand, totalizing narratives, including a grand feminist alternative to science. FemaleMan©

participates in the narratives of science and makes science
a site for feminist technoscience, but not by constructing
a new grand narrative. FemaleMan© is 'about the contingent and disrupted foundational category of woman, dop-
pelganger to the coherent, bright son called man'.[11] The
many voices of FemaleMan© will be both more democratic and less prone to closure than any essentialist discourse.
In Haraway's hands, feminist standpoints of hybridities
become consciously chosen political and social locations,
a range of possible vantage-points available to men as well
as women. Democracy-enhancing projects will define the
'strong objectivity' of 'self-reflexive' socially embedded
practices. On this basis, witnessing will be truly modest,
because it will involve consideration of the many existing
voices and the construction of new voices.

Haraway chides malestream science studies scholars for
their ignorance of this feminist science critique, as well as
for their failure to engage with semiotics, visual culture,
and narrative practice in feminist, post-colonial, post-
structuralist theory. As a result, science studies tend to
treat gender and race as empirical questions, of the absence
or presence of identifiable persons at the scene of action.
That is, the categories of race, class and gender are
deployed in a static, functionalist way. Haraway emphasizes that these categories should not be thought of as
existing independently of technoscience, but rather as
constituted in its practices. Her approach treats these
categories as fluid, dynamic and relational: as 'racial
formation, gender-in-the-making, the forging of class, and
the discursive production of sexuality *through the constitutive practices of technoscience production themselves*'.[12]
Thus Haraway's project is to queer the modest witness 'so
that s/he is constituted in the furnace of technoscientific
practice as a self-aware, accountable, anti-racist Female-
Man©, one of the proliferating, uncivil, late-twentieth-
century children of the early modern *haec vir* and *hic
mulier*'.[13]

OncoMouse™: Technologizing Life and Reprogramming Nature

Haraway's stress on femininity and masculinity, and nature and culture, as inherently relational, highly contextualized concepts is neither novel nor unique to post-structuralism. Rather, it echoes the way gender has come to be theorized over the past two decades within feminist theory. What is particularly valuable for feminism, however, is the way that Haraway applies her relentless deconstructionist method to the operation of the 'natural' as a domain of foundational cultural practice. More than any other thinker, she prompts us to consider the cultural implications of the destabilization of our entrenched Enlightenment distinctions between human, animal and machine. For Haraway, technoscience is a cultural activity that invents Nature, and constructs the nature–culture axis as a classificatory process. This has been the key mechanism for constituting what women are. For feminists, then, the collapse of these oppressive binaries – nature/society, animal/man, human/machine, subject/object, machine/organism, metaphor/materiality – is liberating. With the advent of cybertechnology, women gain the power to transcend the biological body and redefine themselves outside the historical categories of woman, other, object. The laws of nature and biology, as the basis for gender difference and inequality, have finally lost their authority.

The use of the term 'cyborg' to describe a human–machine amalgam originated during the Cold War. It was coined by Manfred Clynes and Nathan Kline in *Astronautics* (1960) for their imagined man–machine hybrid who could survive in extraterrestrial environments. NASA, which needed an enhanced man for space exploration, sponsored their work. According to the original conception, the cybernetic organisms would remain human in a Cartesian sense; their bodies (like machines) would be altered, whilst their minds could continue their scientific research. At that time, Clynes's view was that 'the cyborg, *per se* – talking now of men and women who have altered themselves in various cyborgian ways – in no way has that altered their sexuality'.[14] Haraway takes this idea to a different plane by claiming that the cyborg creature fundamentally redefines what it is to be human, and thus can potentially exist in a world without gender categories. For Haraway, rupturing the ontological divide between living organisms and dead artefacts necessarily challenges gender dualisms.

Modest_Witness provides a compelling account of how developments in the biotechnologies and genetic engineering are reconfiguring our very notion of life itself. The fact that life is literally being redesigned in the scientific laboratory has profound cultural consequences. Our long-standing, taken-for-granted ideas about the relationship between nature and culture, upon which our very notion of what it is to be human depends, are undergoing a radical transformation.

The figure of the OncoMouse™ is at the centre of this narrative about the commercialization or 'branding' of nature that has occurred with the patenting of life forms. OncoMouse™ is a trade-marked 'product'; a living animal used for breast cancer research, it has been genetically manipulated to have a higher propensity to develop cancer. The trade mark is owned by Harvard University, and its exploitation was initially in the hands of DuPont. Haraway uses this icon, the first living creature to be trade-marked, to represent symbolically and materially where the categories of nature and culture implode. 'Defined by a spliced genome, identified with a spliced name, patented, and trademarked, OncoMouse™ is paradigmatic of nature enterprised up.'[15] It is a product of the *nature of no nature* – that is, naturalized technoscience. Genetic engineering produces nature (a mouse) that is not nature, but technoscience. Free enterprise (Nature™) hereby becomes a natural act.

Pause for a moment to consider the unfolding logistical nightmare that is the consequence of the revolution in genomics. According to a report in *Nature*, tens of millions of mutant mice will be needed over the next two or three decades to turn the raw sequence data generated by the Human Genome Project into functional information.[16] British scientists are already genetically modifying half a million animals a year. Although sheep, goats, cattle, pigs, rabbits, birds, poultry and cats are being used, most of the animals altered for research are mice. The spectre is raised of a looming space and financial crisis caused by the need to house and feed these animals as laboratories across the world overflow with mutant mice. There is no doubt that Haraway's choice of OncoMouse™ as emblematic of the new genetics was inspired.

One aspect of Haraway's argument has much in common with radical science or neo-Marxist analyses of science, which see technoscience as increasingly subject to the processes of commodification and capital accumulation. The boundaries between independent university research and industry become blurred, and scientific knowledge becomes intellectual property, as multinational corporations invest unprecedented amounts in biotechnology in their insatiable drive for profit. Indeed, Haraway explicitly draws on the Marxist concept of commodity fetishism to describe how genes, 'those 24-karat-gold macromolecular things-in-themselves', become reified – that is, sources of value in themselves.[17] The global capitalist economy harnesses science to extend the reach of private property to every sphere of life. OncoMouse™, then, is the product of capitalist exploitation.

However, OncoMouse™ is also a cyborg, and in response to this hybridization of nature and culture, Haraway's enthusiasm for cyborg possibilities is tempered with anxiety. OncoMouse™ is a troubling figure, and Haraway is 'fundamentally unresolved' about the moral questions posed by the suffering of animals in experiments. Like so many of us, she is ambivalent because

OncoMouse™ may help to deliver a cure for breast cancer, a disease that kills around 40,000 women a year in the USA alone. In this context she wants both to defend modern science 'evaluated by canons of strong objectivity' and to be science's most radical critic, seeing all knowledges as contingent, situated and located.

Haraway sees a connection between OncoMouse™ and the small animals placed in Boyle's glass jars whose death allowed modest witnesses to attest to the evacuation of the air by the air pump. She makes this connection in the context of her discussion of paintings by Lynn Randolph that accompany Part One of *Modest_Witness*. A breasted OncoMouse™ is portrayed wearing a crown of thorns before the eyes of witnesses: 'this mouse is a figure in secularized Christian salvation history and in the linked narratives of the Scientific Revolution and the New World Order – with their promises of progress; cures; profit; and, if not of eternal life, then at least of life itself'.[18] The passion of OncoMouse™ is a metaphor for the suffering of laboratory animals and the linkages between cyborgs and human interests. Haraway suggests that a politics of hybridity would address the ethics of technoscience. FemaleMan© would knowingly (and in transgenic love) meet OncoMouse™. Haraway accepts the ethical questions raised by eco-feminists, but places them in a more complex context of class and race. In a situation where death rates from breast cancer among African American women in the USA increased by 21 per cent between 1980 and 1991, but remained static for white women, Haraway says: 'the question I want to ask my sibling species, a breast-endowed cyborg like me, is simple: *Cui bono*? For whom does OncoMouse™ live and die? ... Does s/he contribute to deeper equality, keener appreciation of heterogeneous multiplicity, and stronger accountability for livable worlds?'[19]

There is a tension between Haraway's reading of the OncoMouse™ and her more generic use of the cyborg figure. Her cyborg refers to a real, existing compound of the biological and the artefactual, *and* to the mythic protagonist for a new, anti-essentialist feminist subjectivity. Her belief in, and enjoyment of, science and scientific endeavour are apparent in the discussion of these dilemmas; but when faced with a real cyborg, she is not as keen as when contemplating fictional representations or theoretical possibilities.

Send in the Cyborgs

In her more usual postmodern authorial voice, Haraway sees the cyborg as emblematic of a post-gender world which we can now inhabit, and for the most part this is how her work has been interpreted. In this section I want to consider some of the ways in which Haraway's work has been taken up, and where this has taken feminist theory. Does it make sense to claim that we are all cyborgs now? And how subversive is this? In a literal sense, human beings have been prosthetically enhanced in one way or another for centuries, from spectacles to artificial limbs. Is every old-age pensioner with a pace-maker, or organ transplant recipient, a cyborg? I remain unconvinced that a combination of informatics and biogenetics has made the boundary between organisms and machines irrelevant, let alone generated a new ontological status for the species. Our anguished ethical debates over, for example, organ donations and transplants, reflect precisely the importance to people of their bodily integrity, rather than their cyborg-like quality.

Neither is modification of the human body necessarily subversive of the established gender order. From transgender operations literally turning women into men, or vice versa, to cosmetic surgery, surgical procedures are used precisely to reinforce gender stereotypes rather than subvert them. For example, in the past thirty years, approximately two million American women have augmented the size of their breasts with prostheses. For men, the most common augmentation practice is probably the use of steroids such as testosterone for muscular body building. Indeed, the continuing controversy over athletes taking performance-enhancing drugs demonstrates our ambivalence about the boundaries between human and machine. The world-wide enthusiasm for professional sports is strongly based on the value people attach to competition based on the pursuit of excellence through hard work and the development of skills. Taking drugs to gain an advantage is understood to be cheating, and is a shameful accusation in sport because it undermines our trust in the authentic ability of the human athlete. And yet, the practice is clearly endemic at the international level, and people delight in the record-breaking feats of physical prowess that it delivers. Elite athletes may well be cyborgs, but the consequences of this for popular access to sport are uncertain.

The cyborg has fired the feminist imagination. It crystallizes our pleasure in, desire for, and anxiety about technological transcendence. Perhaps this, and the infinite flexibility of what has become the postmodern icon, explains its rhetorical force. Indeed, so ubiquitous is the cyborg figure in popular culture, science fiction books and films, and academic writing that – perhaps, appropriately – it has taken on a life of its own, well beyond Haraway's original conception.

Whereas for Haraway, the cyborg is an ironic political myth with the potential to regenerate socialist feminism, her followers have been drawn to the cyborg for its discursive possibilities. Indeed, while Haraway's cyborg symbolizes a non-holistic, non-universalizing vision for feminist strategies, it has been taken up within cyberfeminism as the symbol of an essential female being. This reflects the fact that Haraway's acolytes tend not to share her firm grounding in the history and social studies of science. In Haraway's hands, the material-semiotic practice of technoscience is a subtle interpretative method that avoids the twin pitfalls of idealism and relativism. Indeed, she is acutely aware of the dangers of being cast as a relativist in the context of the academic 'Science Wars' in the USA, where there is a concerted attack on the discipline of science studies.[20] The same cannot be said for her numerous followers. As Judith Squires expresses it, 'whilst for Haraway cyborg imagery suggests positive new ways of negotiating complex material differences, for others it offers the option of transcending them altogether; of leaving the messy world of material politics behind and entering a post-political utopia of infinite possibility'.[21]

The lived technoscientific reality of cyborgs has taken second place to their treatment as fictional discourse. Whereas Haraway is attuned to the 'fictional' narratives of real science, her followers are more interested in the elaboration of science fictions. There has been a burgeoning feminist literature analysing the key role of gender figurations in science fiction texts. 'Science fiction has become perhaps the quintessential genre of postmodernity in its characteristic representations of futuristic "tomorroworlds", inhabited by aliens, monsters and cyborgs which draw attention to artificiality, simulation and the constructed "otherness" of identity.'[22] Within this literature there is a great deal of debate about whether cyborg images are oppositional, utopian, androgynous hybrids, as in Haraway's lexicon, or whether they reinforce gender stereotypes. In some contexts they celebrate fantasies of superhuman invulnerability. Haraway herself is ever sensitive to the cyborg's ambiguous nature, its dark side as well as its emancipatory potential, reminding us that cyborgs are 'the illegitimate offspring of militarism and patriarchal capitalism'. She is perhaps less attuned to the tainted history of the concept of hybridity, implicated as it is with colonial science projects of the nineteenth century.[23]

The machine that transcends its programming and becomes autonomous is a common figure in contemporary science fiction. This recurring story about how we have lost control over, and are even destroyed by, the machine we have created is the stuff of our collective unconscious and our nightmares about the future. The myth of modern science monsters is usually traced back to Mary Shelley's *Frankenstein*. Emerging almost 200 years ago, Frankenstein's monster appears as monstrous precisely because he/it violates the boundaries between human and non-human. Haraway subverts the horror of this classic tale, embracing hybridity and appropriating the transgressive monstrous otherness. As one of her admirers puts it, 'The cyborg can be reclaimed again, and again, from patriarchal image-making. It can keep a foot in silicon and a foot in carbon; it can run on blood and electricity. It can walk any street in the hope that it will be protected by its ambiguity. It may be wrong, and the risks are great, but it is an agent for fusing embodied, situated knowledge, and powerful fantasy.'[24]

Alas, cyborg images do not always live up to their claim of rupturing the boundary between human and machine, or between women and men. Visual representations of the cyborg in Hollywood science fiction films rarely challenge traditional, Western stereotypes of gendered or racial bodily difference. The heavily sexualized lycra-clad blonde female body wielding a huge weapon is all too familiar. Cybernetic theories of postmodernity tend to ignore the extent to which the cyborg image has already been culturally appropriated in popular forms. As Anne Balsamo argues in her analysis of film and literature, 'the dominant representation of cyborgs reinserts us into dominant ideology by reaffirming bourgeois notions of human, machine and femininity'.[25]

We therefore need to beware of focusing on the cyborg image as a utopian aspirational icon in the service of feminism. It is true that, like feminist analysis, the ironic cyborg vision profoundly disrupts contemporary ideas about the human body. The bionic being defies conventional notions of the body as the site of essential, unified, natural identity. It allows women's bodies to carry a multiplicity of meanings and shifting identities. For many feminists, cyborg images are invigorating and open up productive ways of thinking about subjectivity, gender and the materiality of the physical body. However, real women do live physical difference in the flesh, and my sense is that too much enthusiasm for the cyborg may lead us into a theoretical cul-de-sac. Ironically, while post-modern hybrids breed fertile imaginings, the hybrid progeny of cross-bred animal species are, as every scientist knows, sterile.

Cyborg images can easily be reinscribed in traditional dualisms as part of a romantic narrative about salvation from technology. Indeed, Ronald Reagan was prescient in adopting images from the *Star Wars* film in support of the Strategic Defense Initiative. When Reagan announced his proposal in 1983, he drew on language and images from the film to justify his controversial defence plans, even referring to the Soviet Union as the 'evil empire'. The defence programme came to be known as 'Star Wars', and Reagan brilliantly succeeded in mobilizing images from one of the most popular movies in American history for his own political purposes. The film's creator George Lucas in fact intended the film to be read in the opposite way, with the USA as the evil empire. In today's new world order, the missile defence shield advocated by the Bush Administration has come to be known as the 'Son of Star Wars' and will be responsible for 'homeland' security. The President's war rhetoric, referring to states that allegedly support terrorism as constituting an 'axis of evil', continues this theme.

There is nothing inherently progressive about a cyborgian identification with machines. Indeed, one of the long-standing themes of feminist writing on warfare has been the identification of men and masculinity with the technology of destruction. Sexual imagery has always been part of the world of warfare, and both the military itself and arms manufacturers exploit the phallic imagery and promise of virility that their weapons so conveniently suggest. The story of the development of the atomic bomb vividly illustrates the intensity of the psychological bond with the bomb amongst the scientists who were involved.[26]

One cannot fully comprehend the invention and use of the bomb without appreciating the sense of merger and the loss of boundaries between the men involved and the sublime bomb: 'to the extent that each came to represent – to support, enhance, and speak for – the other'.[27]

The account of the Los Alamos physicists' reaction to the dropping of the bomb on Hiroshima makes particularly chilling reading. Prominent scientists recalled the exultation, celebration and pride they felt in the effectiveness of the weapon, how Oppenheimer was cheered by the entire staff of the laboratory like a 'prize fighter'. 'The only reaction I remember', Richard Feynman recalls, 'was a very considerable elation and excitement. . . . I was involved in this happy thing, drinking and drunk, sitting on the bonnet of a jeep and playing drums, excitement running all over Los Alamos at the same time as the people were dying and struggling in Hiroshima.'[28] Although the principal reason for the establishment of the Manhattan Project was the fear that Nazi Germany would develop atomic weapons, work on the bomb actually intensified after Nazi Germany had surrendered to the Allied armies. What is striking is the sheer joy experienced by this group of male inventors in achieving technological perfection. Certainly their cyborgian identification with the bomb, a transcendent blending of self and machine, makes for disturbing reading.

It is worth recalling that a major part of Haraway's earlier 'A manifesto for cyborgs' addressed the nature of work in global capitalism. There, she argued that 'hybrid' identities were being generalized in the new industrial revolution characterized by the feminization and de-skilling of traditional work. The main deployment of cyborgs around the world today is, indeed, the million or so robots used in the production of cars. Here robots displace human labour.

Much recent feminist writing has emphasized the making of the body through biotechnology and genetic engineering, neglecting other crucial spheres in which the body and gender identity are formed and performed. The workplace is one such site, but its importance is attenuated in Haraway's later work, and absent in that of her followers. The honed, machine-like cyborg body evokes the hypermasculine worker of manufacturing capitalism, but the collapse of physically demanding work is associated with a new obese body, in stark contrast to the kind of body imagined in the figure of the cyborg. Similarly, the feminization of work is not so much about a new cyborg identity, but rather reflects burgeoning demand for service workers with conventional feminine qualities. No wonder, then, that the patriarchal promise of technological progress in the 'military–post-industrial complex' has been the subject of a long and extensive critique within several fields of feminist scholarship.

Conclusion

Throughout her work there is a tension between Haraway the modernist and Haraway the postmodernist. She urges us to celebrate contradiction, inconsistency and fragmentation, and the openness of her writing to a variety of readings is intentional. This can sometimes make Haraway difficult to interpret. Moreover, her rhetorical method and eclectic reference points, ranging from scientific texts to advertisements, paintings, science fiction plots, and her own experiences, assumes a reader who is familiar with North American culture. While such readers often find Haraway's lyrical, irreverent, freely associative ironic style inspiring, readers without the appropriate cultural capital are as likely to find it infuriatingly obscure and impenetrable. That many feminists feel excluded by Haraway's writing style is particularly unfortunate, given that a major theme of her work is the extent to which women are marginalized from scientific discourse.

Perhaps the postmodern euphoria about hybridization and the defeat of essentialisms is itself a culturally specific knowledge practice of the privileged global elite, the only ones who will have access to expensive technoscientific tools for constructing new identities. Indeed, Haraway's attribution of such transformative power to new technologies reflects a very American fascination with technological progress. The narrative of technology redefining reality is, after all, a powerful one with a long lineage. Previous technological innovations like the telephone and electricity were also seen at the time, with some justification, as harbingers of a new social order. One is reluctant to suggest that such an astute science studies critic has fallen prey to technological determinism, but the cyborg prescription for progressive politics does place enormous weight on technoscience as the motor of women's liberation.

Haraway's work takes a modernist turn when she discourses on the plight of African American women, the exploitation of women workers in the global economy, and the missing babies of Brazil. These accounts all rely on official statistics and conventional sociological categories of gender, race and class. The politics that informs Haraway's writing in this context is socialist-feminist, focused on real women's experience of structural domination. Here radical cultural deconstructionism gives way to a causal argument about the existence of institutional and structural effects, and she invokes a yearning for 'knowledge, freedom, and justice in the world of consequential facts'. Like many feminist postmodernists, she at one moment destabilizes the categories of woman and gender, and at the next moment appeals to meta-narratives of justice. She is keenly aware that she needs the category of woman, as well as the tool of statistics, to do politics: 'demanding the competent staffing and funding of the bureaus that produce reliable statistics . . . is indispensable to feminist technoscientific politics'.[29] Yet such statements sit rather uneasily with her emphasis on the impossibility of distinguishing between the material and the metaphorical, between fact and fiction.

Paradoxically, Haraway presents a rather totalizing view of the combination of biotechnology and communication technology as all-powerful in defining who and what we are and as our salvation. She veers between an over-determined view of patriarchal capitalist reproduction and a fantasist vanguardism based on a fixation with cutting-edge technology. But why should feminists be pushed into choosing between the cyborg solution and the goddess solution, 'between a holistic, tree-identified, essentialist utopian feminism and a technologically savvy, cyber-identified anti-essentialist survivalism'?[30] This dichotomous opposition caricatures feminism, ignoring other forms of critical feminist technoscience research, politics and practice that are acutely aware of the dangers of biological essentialisms.

When Haraway does provide a practical example of the technoscientific politics she supports, it is the consensus conference model of technology assessment pioneered in Denmark and now widely adopted in Europe. In this model, panels of ordinary citizens, rather than experts, regularly meet over a period of time to debate government technology policy with a broad range of stake-holders. The model encourages broad public education and participation in determining the value of scientific research for society. While social-democratic models of citizen consultations and audits are an admirable and welcome advance, they are a strangely pedestrian exemplar of cyborg radicalism.

Haraway's emphasis on playfulness and pleasure, as well as engagement and commitment, in technoscientific politics is at once seductive and perplexing. She wants feminists to be more involved in the meaning-making processes of technoscience, and her cultural deconstruction strategy provides us with powerful tools for achieving this. However, in my view, her appositely named 'material-semiotic' approach, which promises to reconcile socialist feminism with postmodernism, strains at the seams. Semiotic analysis takes precedence over materialist aspects of technoscientific practice and politics. Haraway's emphasis on the empowering effects of playful deconstruction, providing us with a sense of agency and hope, has such appeal because for many women the everyday experience of technological change tends to be one of constraint, surveillance, confusion and lack of control. But opening up spaces or playing is a limited form of politics. At times, Haraway loses a sense of how feminists could act to change, or at least redirect technologies, rather than just reconfiguring them in our writings. One is left wondering, with Maureen McNeil, if 'preoccupation with textual and figurative revisioning allowed us to glaze over the political working through required to transform technoscience'.[31] Certainly, Haraway is much stronger at providing evocative figurations of a new feminist subjectivity than she is at providing guidelines for a practical emancipatory politics.

− 5 −

Metaphor and Materiality

There is no 'place' for women in these networks, only geometries of difference and contradiction crucial to women's cyborg identities. If we learn how to read these webs of power and social life, we might learn new couplings, new coalitions.

Donna Haraway, *Simians, Cyborgs, and Women*

In this book I have explored the complex and often fraught relationship between feminism and technoscience. Technology is an intimate presence in our lives and increasingly defines who we are and how we live. Just as the typewriter and the automobile were icons of freedom for women in the discourse of modernity that presaged first-wave feminism, so cyberspace and cyborgs have become ubiquitous postmodern symbols for feminism today.

Women's lives have changed irrevocably during the twentieth century, rendering traditional sex roles increasingly untenable. Dramatic advances in technology, the challenge of feminism, and consciousness of the mutating character of the natural world have prompted visionary thinking. Feminist theorists have asked whether mass digitalization will finally sever the link between technology and male privilege – indeed whether new technologies have undergone a sex change. Yet, even as this question is contemplated, there is a suspicion that existing societal patterns of inequality are being reproduced in a new technological guise.

Feminist theories of the woman–machine relationship have long oscillated between pessimistic fatalism and utopian optimism. The same technological innovations have been categorically rejected as oppressive to women and uncritically embraced as inherently liberating. At the heart of these deliberations lies a concern with the connection between gender and technology. What has been lacking is a coherent theoretical framework that allows us to engage with the process of technical change as integral to the renegotiation of gender power relations. I think this is worth striving for, even while recognizing that knowledge is situated, and theories come to life and have meaning only in specific local contexts of practical activity.

The technofeminist approach I outline in this final chapter fuses the insights of cyborg feminism with those of a constructivist theory of technology. This position eschews both the lingering tendency to view technology as necessarily patriarchal and the temptation to essentialize gender. The theory of technofeminism builds on the insights of cyborg feminism, but grounds it firmly in a thoroughgoing materialist approach to the social studies of technology, including its own role in those studies. In this way, technofeminism also offers a more thoroughgoing critique of mainstream science and technology studies.

I have outlined the problems that feminists have encountered in adopting and adapting the social studies of science and technology approaches in chapter 2, so I will not rehearse them here. But I want to reiterate that they – for example, actor-network analyses – have often been blind to gender, race, religion, class, sexuality and other axes of social difference. The turn from macro-structural to ethnographic approaches has served as a compelling critique of a static notion of social interests, but the 'doing' of gender, both by male academics and by those they study, is rarely considered. As researchers, many fail to recognize that women's absence from the sociotechnical network does not mean that it is a gender-free zone. The network certainly has a gender politics. For this to become visible, the concept of the sociotechnical network needs to be extended.

In this final chapter, I argue for a recognition that gender and technoscience are mutually constitutive, and explain how this opens up fresh possibilities for feminist scholarship and action. I shall show that beneath a discourse of a gender-neutral sociotechnical network there is frequently to be found the hidden agency of new social movements, many of which are feminist in character, or have been inspired by feminism.

Changing Technologies, Changing Subjectivities

I began the book with a discussion of early feminist writing on gender and technology, much of which adopted a pessimistic tone. Originating from a liberal concern with women's historical exclusion from technical skills and careers, this perspective evolved into an analysis of the masculine character of technology itself. Technology was seen as a key source of male power, encompassing technologies of human biological reproduction and those of the workplace. Socialist and radical feminism emphasized the social relations of technology, and delivered a compelling critique of popular and sociological arguments that were (and still are) characterized by technological determinism. Technology was seen as socially shaped, but shaped by men to the exclusion of women. Problems of essentialism remained in much of this writing, leading to an over-emphasis on the intransigent aspects of patriarchal structures and norms embedded in technology. This scholarship was however much more sophisticated than is now acknowledged and, as I have suggested in chapter 1, was prescient about developments in biotechnology and the computerization of work.

Much of this literature made a strong link between capitalism and patriarchy, seeing class and gender as bound together in the social relations of capitalism. For most social theorists, capitalist industrial society was characterized by sharp divisions between manual and non-manual work, between valued employment and devalued, privatized work in households, and gender-segregated employment patterns. However, as I argued, this dominant view of capitalism and its future development was in the process of breaking down, and the trends in computerization and biotechnology that socialist and radical feminists had identified were increasingly being associated with a fundamental change in capitalism itself. According to theories of post-industrial society, the old hierarchies were disintegrating and being replaced by less rigid, more flexible networks. At the same time, with rising standards of living, identities formed within consumption seemed to be becoming more important than those formed within the social relations of work and production. Theorists like Anthony Giddens and Ulrich Beck have argued that a new process of 'individualization' is undermining traditional sources of identity and solidarity, such as gender, local neighbourhood and class. For them, individuals in a post-industrial society are becoming 'reflexively aware', taking responsibility for their own biographies and 'choosing' life-styles and identities.

Reflecting more general trends in social theory, feminists have become increasingly uneasy with the negative cast of the debates about technology and society. They have warmed to information, communication and biotechnologies as being fundamentally transformative, unlike previous technologies. Theories of the global, networked, knowledge society see these technologies as revolutionary in their impact, providing the basis for a new information age. Cyberfeminists have been particularly influenced by these ideas and, more generally, the 'cultural turn' in social theory. The virtuality of cyberspace and the Internet is seen as ending the embodied basis for sex difference and facilitating a multiplicity of innovative subjectivities. In the wired world, traditional hierarchies are replaced by horizontal, diffuse, flexible networks that have more affinity with women's values and ways of being than with men's. Here, I suggest, we have a technological and biological determinism in a new postmodern guise, this time as cyberculture in and of itself freeing women.

The optimistic register of such feminisms, stressing women's agency and capacity for empowerment, resonates with a new generation of women who live in a world of much greater sex equality. That a strong current of Seventies feminism sought to reject technology as malevolent is now seen as fanciful. Wired women in cyber-cafes, experimenting with new media, clutching mobile phones, are immersed in science fiction and their imaginary worlds. It presents a seductive image for a culture with an insatiable appetite for novelty. The possibilities of reinventing the self and the body, like cyborgs in cyberspace, and the prosthetic potential of biotechnologies, have reinvigorated our thinking. But the sometimes tenuous link between visceral, lived gender relations and the experience of virtual voyages has led many to desire a more materialist analysis of gender and technology.

To move forward, we first need to bridge the common polarization in social theory between metaphor and materiality. Technology must be understood as part of the social fabric that holds society together; it is never merely technical or social. Rather, technology is always a socio-material product – a seamless web or network combining artefacts, people, organizations, cultural meanings and knowledge. It follows that technological change is a contingent and heterogeneous process in which technology and society are mutually constituted. Indeed, the linear model of innovation, diffusion and use has given way to the idea that technology is never a finished product. Long after artefacts leave the research laboratory, they continue to evolve in everyday practices of use. The interpretative flexibility of technology means that the possibility always exists for a technology and its effects to be otherwise. If society is co-produced with technology, it is imperative to explore the effects of gender power relations on design and innovation, as well as the impact of technological change on the sexes. An emerging technofeminism conceives of a mutually shaping relationship between gender and technology, in which technology is both a source and a consequence of gender relations. In other words, gender relations can be thought of as materialized in technology, and masculinity and femininity in turn acquire their meaning and character through their enrolment and embeddedness in working machines. Such an approach shares the constructivist conception of technology as a sociotechnical network, and recognizes the need to integrate the material, discursive and social elements of technoscientific practice.

Feminist scholarship has been critical in exposing the gender-blindness of mainstream technoscience studies. Donna Haraway's contribution has been key, continuing the tradition of socialist-feminist inquiry into the possibilities that technoscience offers women. I have argued that her material-semiotic approach moves beyond the limitations of cyberfeminism, with its tendency to biological essentialism. The issue is no longer whether to accept or oppose technoscience, but rather how to engage strategically with technoscience while at the same time being its chief critic. Haraway's spotlight on the life sciences raises crucial issues of our time – in particular, whether the boundaries between nature and culture and between humans and machines, which have been an underlying premise of the Enlightenment world-view, can be sustained and, if not, what the consequences are for our conception of humanness and the gendered body.

While broadly sympathetic with Haraway's unique attempt to bridge socialist and postmodern feminism, I have argued that her 'cyborg solution' risks fetishizing new technologies. Her piercing analysis of the interconnections between capitalism, patriarchy and technoscience sits uneasily with her belief in a radical discourse of discontinuity and the emancipatory potential of advanced technologies. At times, the cyborg solution comes dangerously close to endorsing cyberfeminism's embrace of all technological innovations *per se*. While Haraway's lively textual deconstruction is appealing, as is her optimism, her focus on gender-as-it-could-be loses sight of the pervasive and relatively obdurate gender structure of sociotechnical relations. In the end, Haraway and those influenced by her give semiotics precedence over materialist aspects of technoscience.

Towards Technofeminism

Throughout this book, I have called into question the implicit division between cutting-edge technologies and existing technologies. I have suggested that all technologies be properly characterized as contingent and open, expressing the networks of social relations in which they are embedded. With this in mind, we will be less inclined to identify technology itself as the source of positive or negative change, and will concentrate instead upon the changing social relationships within which technologies are embedded and how technologies may facilitate or constrain those relationships.

I have frequently drawn on examples from earlier technologies to emphasize the heterogeneity of technological innovation. I now want to look in more detail at examples of digital technologies and their sociotechnical networks in order to draw the different threads of my argument together. I shall argue that while these technologies are different in important respects from those that preceded them, the social networks in which technologies are embedded have also changed. Importantly, they have changed their character and identities in part as a consequence of feminist politics. Technological advances do open up new possibilities because some women are better placed to occupy the new spaces, and are less likely to regard machinery as a male domain.

This is in no small measure due to the sustained efforts of liberal feminists over the past thirty years. International feminist networks, such as Gender and Science and Technology (GASAT), have campaigned to encourage women and girls into scientific and technical education and employment. Workshops to encourage women to take up computing became widespread, and the analogy between the binary logic of writing software and knitting patterns was drawn to feminize this skill. Around the world, government policies reflect these concerns. Special programmes have been devised to encourage girls to pursue mathematics and technical subjects in schools. The standard engineering curriculum has also been targeted as a key barrier to changing the sex composition of students.

These efforts are continuing, and are an established feature of formal women's equality strategies. Progress has been halting. A recent report comparing six countries, including the USA, found that women are generally under-represented among graduates in the information technology, electronics and communications-related subjects, despite the fact that they form the majority of university graduates overall.[1] In the USA, for example, women were particularly under-represented among graduates in computer and information science (33 per cent) and engineering (20 per cent). At the doctoral level, in computer and information science, women accounted for but 19 per cent of degrees, and in engineering, only 17 per cent. The exception is the biological sciences, where women continue to be well represented.

This imbalance in women's and girl's educational choices has major repercussions because employment in the information technology, electronics and communications sector is graduate-intensive. It is reflected in women's low participation in these occupations across the US economy, which declined from 37 per cent in 1993 to 28 per cent at the start of the twenty-first century. Where women are relatively well represented is in the lower-status occupations, such as telephone operators, data processing equipment installers and repairers, and communications equipment operators. By contrast, male graduates are heavily concentrated among computer systems analysts and scientists, computer science teachers, computer programmers, operations and systems researchers and analysts, and broadcast equipment operators.[2]

Such relatively stubborn sex-stereotyping is particularly intriguing given the feminization of higher education and work which has seen, for example, women entering law, medicine and business schools in unprecedented numbers. Moreover, it is highly irrational in a post-industrial society, whose economy is reputedly based on investment in human rather than physical capital. To paraphrase Manuel Castells, the key to success in the Network Society is self-programmable labour – knowledge workers who are highly educated, talented, flexible, innovative and autonomous. Whereas the key technologies of the industrial era were largely muscle-enhancing, information technologies are considered to be brain-enhancing.

So, the traditional basis for men's domination of scientific, engineering and technical institutions has been well and truly undermined. Yet women still face considerable barriers when they attempt to pursue a professional or managerial career in technoscience. It is necessary therefore to revisit the liberal feminist agenda of equal opportunities, and not to regard it simply as superseded. Women are missing out on good jobs in the knowledge economy, thereby impeding their financial independence. While the labour market remains so strongly sex-segregated and marked by a gender pay gap, social justice in employment will continue to elude us.

Moreover, a democratic commitment to equality between the sexes must go beyond the objective of equal pay. What has been missing from much of the debate about getting women into technoscience is that their under-representation profoundly affects how the world is made. Every aspect of our lives is touched by sociotechnical systems, and unless women are in the engine-rooms of technological production, we cannot get our hands on the levers of power. This is the insight that technofeminism brings to these debates. I believe that there is room for an effective politics around gaining access to technoscientific work and institutions. There are opportunities for disruption. The involvement of more women in scientific and technological work, in technology policy, education and so on may bring significant advances in redesigning technology. It would also both require and constitute a challenge to the male culture of technology.

Understanding the alliance between technoscience and male power involves seeing technology as a culture that expresses and consolidates relations amongst men. Feminist writing has long not only identified the ways in which gender–technology relations are manifest in gender structures and institutions, but also highlighted gender symbols and identities. Men's affinity with technology is integral to the constitution of subject identity for both sexes.

I have written elsewhere about archetypal masculine cultures such as engineering, where mastery over technology is a source of both pleasure and power for the predominantly male profession.[3] This resonates with today's dominant image of IT work: the young, white, male 'nerds' or 'hackers' who enjoy working sixteen-hour days. Indeed, it is rare to see a female face among the dot.com millionaires. The 'cyber-brat pack' for the new millennium – those wealthy and entrepreneurial young guns of the Internet – consists almost entirely of men. The masculine workplace culture of passionate virtuosity, typified by hacker-style work, epitomizes a world of mastery, individualism and non-sensuality. Being in an intimate relationship with a computer is both a substitute for, and a refuge from, the much more uncertain and complex relationships that characterize social life. Writers such as Castells, who eulogize the counterculture hacker origins of the Internet, fail to notice that the culture of computing is predominantly the culture of the white American male. This is not to imply that there is a single form of masculinity. Sexual ideologies are remarkably diverse and fluid, and for some men technical expertise may be as much about their lack of power as a realization of it. It is indubitably the case however that in contemporary Western society, the hegemonic form of masculinity is still strongly associated with technical prowess and power. Feminine identity, on the other hand, has involved being ill-suited to technological pursuits. Entering technical domains has therefore required women to sacrifice major aspects of their gender identity.

A successful career in IT requires navigation of multiple male cultures associated not only with technological work but also with managerial positions, as I have discussed in *Managing Like a Man*.[4] For many women the price is too high. No equivalent sacrifice has been expected of men. Their identification with technology has been taken for granted, women's absence cast as women's problem. But women's problem is men, even though not all men are directly implicated. The challenge is for men who have premissed their masculinity on technical mastery to relinquish their hold on technology and give up the privileges and power that go with this construction of masculinity.

These technoscientific spheres will become more attractive to women when entry does not entail co-option into a world of patriarchal values and behaviour. As the proportion of women engineers grows, for example, the strong relationship between the culture of engineering and hegemonic masculinity will eventually be dismantled. Contemporary feminist criticism has sought to recover the feminine subject by challenging notions of women's passivity and identifying the different ways in which women actively resist and subvert conventional constructions of femininity. Wary of premissing a subjectivity on the commonality of women, postmodern feminism stresses the multiplicity of identities and the desire for self-determination. Such an approach helps to account for different women's mixed and contradictory feelings when encountering technology. It also foregrounds the idea that women want to participate in technoscience on their own terms, and not as surrogate men. Ultimately this depends on transforming gender power relations, which in turn requires changing the nature of work itself. Information and communication technologies offer the possibility of transforming the organization of work, making it more flexible and potentially enabling an easier blend of work and caring responsibilities. Personal computers, fax machines, mobile phones and e-mail mean that the performance of paid work no longer requires personnel to be physically present in the workplace. Mothers, and increasingly fathers too, are tapping into the space-time flexibility this affords to combine employment with child care. A reintegration of work and personal life, involving more sharing of paid work and housework, puts pressure on the traditional institutions of work that are themselves founded on gender inequality. Any move towards more egalitarian domestic arrangements will, in turn, enable women to take their full place in technoscientific work.

As feminists have argued, reordering the work–life balance will require recognizing the 'politics' of time. The different patterns currently found among men and women, and between parents and non-parents, reflect earlier negotiations of employment and personal life in different sociotechnical conditions. However, it is somewhat ironic that the 'imaginary' of new technologies emphasizes how they might liberate time, while the cutting-edge industries associated with them frequently exhibit the long hours associated with particular male work cultures.

At the same time, some women are using biotechnologies to enable them to adopt the male template of uninterrupted work. After all, the construction of women as different from men is a key mechanism whereby male power in the workplace is maintained. Taking the contraceptive Pill, followed by Hormone Replacement Therapy, women are able to avoid the biological characteristics of femininity – namely, menstruation, pregnancy, breastfeeding and menopause. These corporeal processes signal women's difference, and mark them as unsuitable for the global, mobile, elite levels of corporate careers.

Postmodern analyses have correctly identified the body as increasingly a site for capital accumulation, and not just reproduction. New body regimes are seen as a linchpin of personal identity processes. However, much of this writing locates the body as an article in consumer culture, emphasizing the work people do on themselves through purchasing commodities. Cyborg feminism sees these technologies as potentially dissolving the sex/gender nexus in the hybridization of the lived sexed body and machines. Less attention has been given to work organizations as crucial sites in which the doing of gender is routinely accomplished. In this context, it may well be that Haraway's FemaleMan© could serve to sustain rather than undermine patriarchal work cultures. We must not forget that the future is open, and its direction will depend upon the forms of agency that shape it.

We saw earlier how the formation of engineering as a white, male, middle-class profession in the late nineteenth century cemented the gendered definition of technical expertise still familiar today. Muscles, skill, strength, dexterity, rationality and labour time became the preserve of men and important power resources. While the masculine subject was enrolled into this sociotechnical network, standard versions of femininity were simultaneously excluded. Indeed, the tight connection between gender identities inscribed on the body and the emerging networks accounts for their durability. Recent social studies of technology share with post-structuralist feminism an emphasis on the contingent and performative character of the self. As we have seen, the appeal of digital virtuality for postmodern cyberfeminist writing is that it enables women to occupy new discursive positions beyond the dualism of gender. However, while escaping the corporeal body may be an appealing emancipatory strategy, it leaves untouched the gendered distribution of materials and resources that typically afford women less scope for initiatives in the workplace. It also misses the extent to which it is female corporeality that is being socially constructed as the problem, thereby reinforcing the power of masculine norms.

In order to renegotiate the cultural equation between masculinity and technology, technofeminism insists that we must attend to women's and men's concrete sociotechnical practices. A central theme of early feminist writing on technology was the power that men gained through their privileged access to muscle, capability, tools and machinery, 'part of the process by which females are constituted as women'.[5] We stressed that men's physical capacity and tangible skills were not so much due to natural difference, but were largely socially acquired, resulting in sex differences in ways of using the body to perform tasks. Moreover, women's marginalization from technical work has made it more difficult for them to acquire the practical experience and tacit knowledge necessary for expertise and confidence in physical engagement with objects. Rereading this literature now, it is strikingly resonant with current developments in feminist philosophy and sociological theory that stress the embodied character of social identity.[6] Actor-network theory, for example, sees the embodied self as a relational and material phenomenon, an assemblage acquiring its substance through its connections and embeddedness in networks.

Pierre Bourdieu's concepts of habitus and embodied cultural capital are in vogue as a way of grounding cultural theory in a sociology of practice. The habitus of social relations and practices includes machines; but what is less well understood is how machines themselves have a habitus and embody particular forms of cultural capital. Research on information systems and artificial intelligence is increasingly emphasizing the importance of the body in human cognition and behaviour. For example, researchers at the University of Texas in Dallas have created a robot – K-Bot – with a human face, to facilitate interaction between humans and socially intelligent machines.[7] Unlike Andy, the first prototype, K-Bot has a female face, perhaps indicating that women are associated with emotional intelligence. None the less, the emotions that K-Bot can express – from sneering and frowning to smiling – are part of a repertoire of human communication that is highly gendered in terms of its use in social settings, including its use in hierarchy and dominance. The fact that K-Bot is represented as female is potentially about diminishing the threat that intelligent machines might pose to their human creators. It may also reflect the fantasy of systems designers, in a service economy predicated on female labour, who dream of being relieved of the mundane work involved in servicing themselves.[8]

If the gendered self is 'an assemblage of materials', then women's emancipation requires changing the woman–machine relationship to enhance women's capacity for initiatives over machines. In other words, all these streams of argument strengthen the need for women's greater appropriation of tools and technical expertise. Our interest here is the way in which some men can effectively deploy their technical and bodily capital to control technology, and the way in which male bodily capital can become embodied in technology. This point is routinely overlooked in the field of men's studies, which rarely sees sociotechnical relations as central to defining various masculinities. By linking gender to technology, technofeminist perspectives add a new dimension to sociological analyses of gender difference and sexual inequality.

Sociotechnical Practices: Expertise and Agency

The way technologies are encoded with gendered meanings that shape their design and use has been a recurring theme in this book. It is worth briefly reminding ourselves about the process of innovation, outlined in chapter 2. During the design process, the developer maps out a plan for how the technical system will be used. This plan can be thought of as inscribed in the infrastructure. The inscription includes programmes of action for the users, defining roles to be played by users and the artefact or information system. Being inscribed in this way, technology becomes an actant imposing its programmes of action on its users. To be effective, programmes of action need to be inscribed not only in discrete devices, but also in aligned networks of technologies, humans and social institutions.

Of course, actual practice can deviate from the assigned programme of action. The construction of technical arte-facts is not the exclusive domain of inventors and manu-facturers. When studying the use of technical artefacts, one necessarily shifts back and forth between the designer's projected user and the real user, in order to describe this dynamically negotiated process of design. The interpreta-tive flexibility of objects does provide entry points for women to renegotiate sociotechnical networks. Feminist systems developers are also involved in alternative forms of participatory design practice that take women's knowl-edges into account.[9] But for present purposes I want to highlight how the predominance of men in the design process may affect the shape and direction of technologi-cal innovation. It also positions women as *responding* to technologies that are already there.

Let us take the example of the wired house. One of the great paradoxes about domestic technologies is that, despite being universally promoted as saving time, these technologies have been singularly unsuccessful in lessening women's domestic load.[10] We might have hoped that the electronic home would achieve the wholesale elimination of household labour. The smart houses occupied by the very affluent display what high-technology dwellings might offer the family of the future. Magazines like *Wired* and futuristic films present home networking as the back-bone infrastructure of the twenty-first-century life-style.

But it seems that the designers and producers of the technological home, such as the MIT 'House of the Future', have little interest in housework.[11] Home informatics is mainly concerned with the centralized control of heating, lighting, security, information, entertainment and energy consumption in a local network or 'house-brain'.[12] Prototypes of the intelligent house tend to ignore the whole range of functions that come under the umbrella of housework. The target consumer is implicitly the technically interested and entertainment-oriented male, someone in the designer's own image. The smart house is a deeply masculine vision of a house, rather than a home, somewhat like Corbusier's 'machine for living'. The routine neglect of women's knowledge, experience and skills as a resource for technical innovation in the home is symptomatic of the gendered character of the process.

While there would certainly be a commercial market for smart technologies that reduce housework, such as the robotic vacuum cleaner, the variety and complexities of household labour impose limits on its mechanization. Even in the differently ordered world of paid work, robots perform only routine tasks in manufacturing, and personal service work has proved impossible to automate. However, my point here is that even the most visionary futurists have us living in households that, in social rather than technological terms, resemble the households of today. The space-age design effort is directed to a technological fix rather than to envisioning social changes that would see a less gendered allocation of housework and a better balance between working time and family time. The wired home may have much to offer but democracy in the kitchen is not part of the package.

I have argued that the possibilities afforded by technological advances do not inhere in individual artefacts but are contingent upon the networks in which they are located. Once we look beyond the house itself as the site of domestic labour, we immediately see that working women are using their new-found economic independence to buy their way out of housework. Cleaners and child-carers are only part of the story. Most striking is the extent to which women have embraced innovations in market-based alternatives to home-produced meals. Restaurant meals, take-away food, and almost-ready-to-eat goods from the supermarkets are extensively used to reduce the time women spend on domestic tasks.[13] Earlier I described how the microwave oven was seized upon by women, although it was designed for single men. These food technologies have changed the boundaries between the private sphere of the home and the public sphere of production. Despite the significance of this, they have received much less attention from third-wave and post-feminisms than, for example, biotechnologies.[14] However, it may be that these unsung sociotechnical networks have played a key role in transforming gender relations in the home and opening up the public sphere to women.

The telephone is another classic case of how women can actively subvert the original inscription of a technology. Designed by telegraph men for business purposes, the telephone was taken up by women for social functions. Similarly, the business-oriented mobile phone is widely used by women for reasons of personal security and maintenance of contact with the family. While this may be an intrusion of domestic pressure on women into spaces and times where previously they were isolated from it, remote mothering enables women to exist in domestic and work modes simultaneously.

Indeed, early concerns about women being left out of the communications revolution now seem misplaced. A proliferation of mobile phones, the Internet and cyber-cafes are providing new opportunities and outlets for women. This is particularly the case for middle-class women in highly industrialized countries, who are better placed than other groups of women to take advantage of these technologies. More than two-thirds of the Internet's content is, after all, in English. However, the Internet and the mobile phone may ultimately have even greater significance for women in low-income households and communities in the global South. Pay-as-you-go mobiles have enabled hundreds of millions in Africa, Asia and the former Soviet Union to bypass the financial and bureaucratic obstacles of land-line phones and get connected. Around the world, although women still account for a lower proportion of Internet users than men, their share is rapidly rising.

Fear that the globalization of communications leads to homogenization, and reduces sociability and engagement with one's community, is a recurring theme in the literature. But all the signs are that new electronic media can help to build local communities and project them globally. The expansion of cyberspace makes it possible for even small, poorly resourced NGOs to connect with each other and engage in global social efforts. These political activities are an enormous advance for women who were formerly isolated from larger public spheres and cross-national social initiatives. 'We see here the potential transformation of women, "confined" to domestic roles, who can emerge as key actors in global networks without having to leave their work and roles in their communities.'[15] Just as the car increased women's mobility and capacity to participate in public space, so the new media have expanded women's horizons and capacity to connect with networks and campaigns to improve their conditions. To this extent, women are reinterpreting the technologies as tools for political organizing and the means for creation of new feminist communities.

Recognition of these opportunities is not to endorse utopian ideas of cyberspace being gender-free and the key to women's liberation. I remain sceptical of exaggerated claims by cyber-gurus and cyberfeminists about the Internet being the technological basis for a new form of society. Rather, it is to stress that the Internet, like other technologies, is flexible and contains contradictory possibilities. Much has been made of the 'digital divide' producing new forms of social exclusion. Policies to reduce disparities in Internet access, and the acquisition of skills to use these new media, are important. However, a technofeminist perspective points beyond the discourse of the digital divide to the connections between gender inequality and other forms of inequality, which come into view if we examine the broader political and economic basis of the networks that shape and deploy technical systems. Most commentators take the technical architecture of new media, such as the Internet and the Web, as pre-given. The issue for them is one of diffusion. However, most new media configurations are biased towards exclusive electronic spaces for commercial activity. As Saskia Sassen notes, the three properties of digital networks – decentralized access, simultaneity and interconnectivity – have produced strikingly different outcomes in the private, fire-walled sites of global finance from the distributed power of the public-access cyberspaces. In fact, there are trends towards increasing privatization of the Internet, with multiple classes of service and access to information depending upon the ability of users to pay.[16] Network power is not then inherently distributive, as cyberfeminists among others would have us believe. In the hands of multinational corporations and capital markets, it can concentrate power.

Much of the triumphalism about digitization rests on the assumption that we are living in a post-industrial, consumer-based society. There is a widespread belief that production is no longer the organizing principle of contemporary society. The focus has shifted to information, consumption, culture and life-style. However, production has not disappeared, but is being carried out in strikingly novel forms on an increasingly global basis. Much low-skilled, assembly-line work has moved offshore to the Third World, and is performed predominantly by women rather than men. The quintessential product and symbol of the new age, the computer, is often manufactured in precisely this fashion. For a young woman in the West, her silver cell phone is experienced as a liberating extension of her body. The social relations of production that underpin its existence are invisible to her. As material objects, mobile phones have to be mass-produced in factories. Furthermore, along with other electronic devices, such as laptops, they require the scarce mineral Coltan. One of the few places where this can be found is Central Africa, where it is mined under semi-feudal and colonial labour relations, to provide raw product for Western multinational companies. The sharp rise in the price of Coltan on global markets has local effects, accentuating exploitation and conflict among competing militias, with the very specific consequences for women that military conflict brings – namely, rape and prostitution.[17]

A mobile phone then is a very different artefact, depending upon a person's place within the socio-technical network. In tying together these relations of production and consumption, technofeminism not only scrutinizes the emancipatory metaphors, but also seeks to balance this analysis with an equal emphasis on the material realities of a technology's production and use.

It is much remarked upon that anti-corporate globalization protests rely on global new media for their mobilization, as well as enjoying simultaneous broadcast on conventional mass media such as television, radio and newspapers. Electronic space is thus a crucial force for new forms of civic participation. Consumers are using this space to express solidarity with the poorly paid producers of their fashionably branded goods. These initiatives can bypass national states, and create new networks involving historically disadvantaged peoples and groups. Foremost among these are women, who are a dynamic presence in cyberspace.

Indeed, the communications revolution coincides with massive social transformations associated with increasing emancipation of women world-wide, economically, culturally, and politically. Likewise, when we look back at the revolution in contraceptive technologies, we can see that women were not the passive recipients of a 'magic bullet'

delivering sexual liberation. Western women were ready
for the Pill because of other changes to the family and the
economy, which were giving rise to second-wave feminism;
but they had practised contraception long before the
advent of the Pill.[18] Today much is made of innovative biomedical techniques bringing about new family forms and
disrupting traditional blood-based kinship. But developments such as the increased incidence of lesbian mothers
are a product of women's economic independence and
feminist/gay/queer politics, rather than *in vitro* fertilization. The belated emergence of the male Pill similarly
reflects changes in gender politics rather than recent
scientific advances.

In the previous chapter we saw how Haraway decon-
structs the 'modest witness' to the birth of experimental
science as being implicitly a white European male. The
gender critique of scientific knowledge, and the attempt to
regain control over women's bodies, were key to second-
wave feminism. There was a growing disenchantment with
male medical theories and practices. The development and
consolidation of male expertise at women's expense was
splendidly captured in *Witches, Midwives and Nurses: A
History of Women Healers*.[19] As well as being scholarly,
studies such as this inspired new political practices. Collective self-help groups for purposes including contraception,
pregnancy testing and gynaecological self-examination
empowered women in relation to professional medical
control. These initiatives were born of the conviction that
women could develop new kinds of knowledge and skills,
drawing on their own experience and needs, while being
sensitive to racial, class and ethnic differences.

Women have come into medicine in great numbers at all
levels, and now form a critical mass in the biological sciences and as doctors, as well as being the principal consumers of health services. Birthing practices that once had
mothers flat on their backs with their legs in stirrups have
been transformed as a direct result of feminist campaigns
to give women more control. Women have mobilized to

share medical information and compare treatment regimes, challenging deference to medical expertise. They have been quick to seize on the Internet, both as a source of information and as a tool for global exchange, support and political lobbying. For example, the National Breast Cancer Coalition used such means to convince the US Congress to more than double its funding for breast cancer research. These new patient associations are displaying a new militancy, and are demanding a voice in how their conditions are conceptualized, treated and researched. Such networks promote women's agency and increase their capacity to engage in the production of scientific knowledge.

While the grass-roots AIDS treatment movement is now routinely credited with transforming the relationship between patients, disease and medication, it learnt much from the women's health movement of the 1970s. The AIDS movement, however, had a distinct advantage in being dominated by white middle-class men with a degree of political clout, fund-raising capacity and a high proportion of medical and other professionals, unusual for an oppressed group. Examining the gay community's efforts to speed up and direct AIDS treatment from 1987 to 1992, Steven Epstein argues that they succeeded in influencing how scientific research is done by adopting strategies that scientists themselves use. AIDS activists accomplished an identity shift: 'they reconstituted themselves as a new species of expert – as laypeople who could speak credibly about science in dialogues with the scientific research community'.[20] Establishing themselves as the legitimate representatives of the entire HIV-positive population, they became obligatory passage points, standing between researchers and the clinical trials they sought to conduct. Importantly, activists tied their moral and political concerns to epistemological and methodological arguments, using accepted notions of good science to gain credibility and support from scientists and the general public.

Clearly the politics of such coalitions is not without contradictions: primarily the conflict between commercial and public interests. In this case, AIDS activists wanted wider access to health care, including experimental new drug treatments; companies wanted to design and market new, profitable drug treatments. While the negotiation between the two sides did not make the drug companies community-oriented, changes in the approval process did incorporate many of the users' demands. Moreover, the movement's success has had an enduring impact on biomedicine in the USA, enhancing consumers' right to biomedical knowledge and allowing new actors to enter sociotechnical networks of health care. New campaigns linked both to these health movements and to anticapitalist protests have had some success in pressuring pharmaceutical multinationals to waive their patent rights, thereby making life-prolonging HIV/AIDS treatment drugs more affordable for people in developing countries. There women bear the brunt of the epidemic: more than five million young women (between the ages of fourteen and twenty-four) are living with HIV/AIDS in sub-Saharan Africa, and two and a half million young men.

However, the best immunization against AIDS for children is to ensure that girls have the resources to grow up to be financially independent and that boys learn to respect women. Without access to education, land and credit, young women do not have the knowledge or economic power they need to negotiate sexual activity successfully. Condoms and AIDS education are of little use to girls who lack the bargaining power to negotiate safe sex. In Uganda and Senegal – Africa's most heralded successes in stemming the spread of HIV/AIDS – the empowerment of women and girls has been instrumental in changing risky sexual practices.[21] Both countries have opened up access to productive resources to women, starting with girls' education. The lesson from this experience is the importance of empowering women, rather than relying on a technological fix. The idea of the sociotechnical web emphasizes the need to contextualize the meaning, effects and perceived value of technologies, as they vary by culture and country.

While there are enormous differences between women, especially in the developed and developing countries, educating girls may in the end be the universal key to transforming female embodied subjectivities.

Conclusion

One of the ironies of mainstream science and technology studies is that, while its central premiss holds that technoscience is socially shaped and inherently political, there has been a reluctance to consider the implications of its own methodologies. Practitioners act as if their own methodologies are not affected by the social context and have no politics. They do not reflect on how the preponderance of white, privileged, heterosexual men might have framed the field. Paradoxically, under attacks from science wars writers, some science studies authors have taken refuge in conventional social science attitudes of disinterest and disembodiment. Some go as far as to claim the principle of generalized agnosticism, according to which the investigator should not take sides in the technical or social aspects of the controversy being studied.[22]

Feminist scholars have long rejected this 'principle', substituting a reflexivity about the relationship between researchers and the subjects of their research that acknowledges the bond between theory, research and experience. Mainstream authors are much more reluctant to deconstruct their own claims to authority. Legitimating the scientific status of the field has involved erecting a boundary between 'good' science studies and feminist approaches, the common charge being that feminist technoscience has a 'frankly political agenda'.[23]

This is so, but not in the way that the mainstream charges. For technofeminism, politics is an 'always-already' feature of a network, and a feminist politics is a necessary extension of network analysis. Science and technology embody values, and have the potential to embody different values. The strength of feminism is that it is strongly attached to a rigorous social analysis – that is, one that meets certain evidence standards, yet always links research to a political practice of making a difference to the network and its effects. It is this relationship between social analysis and projects of social transformation that marks a fundamental difference between standard technoscience studies and technofeminism.

But can we speak of techno*feminism* in the singular in the midst of an efflorescence of theoretical work contesting and revisioning the categories of gender and sexuality? The emergence of black and post-colonial feminism, for example, has posed a critical challenge to the privileging of the preoccupations and knowledges of white, Western women. As a result, feminist conversations are much more attuned to the different ways women live and experience technoscience, depending on their location.

For all the diversity of feminist voices, however, there is a shared concern with the hierarchical divisions between men and women that order the world we inhabit. I have set out examples of the many different ways in which women's groups and others inspired by feminist political practice have infiltrated and begun to reshape the networks of science and technology. The feminist project may not be finished, but it has made a difference, and, in conjunction with emerging technologies, is creating new spaces for further development of the project. Issues of embedded inequality and privilege recur, and must be addressed. A technofeminist conception of sociotechnical networks enables such connections to be made, from the micro-politics of local activism to the macro-politics of global movements.

The feminist project is incomplete, and some, as we have seen, have responded to the distance we have yet to travel with the kind of pessimism that fosters an essentialist view of technology and its gendered power relations. Cyberfeminists have taken a utopian position, looking to new technologies as in themselves transformative. The problem with both positions is that they assign too much agency to new technology, and not enough to feminist politics. Tech-nofeminism is grounded in the understanding that only we can free ourselves. This makes a feminist politics both pos-sible and necessary. Feminist politics has made a differ-ence, and we can build upon the difference it has made. We do not live in a world that is post-feminist, but we do live in a world that feminism has shaped and will continue to shape.

The denial of feminist politics remains a feature of main-stream discourses, both academic and everyday, and it would be cruelly ironic if our own frustrations with what remains to be done should contribute to our own margin-alization. Especially since feminist politics remains one of the major sources of contestation of inequality and privi-lege in a world where it can frequently seem as if gains previously won might easily be lost.

For example, the juxtaposition of scientific expertise with lay citizens' knowledge has become a mainstream political issue in today's accident-prone world. In contrast to the bright future predicted by information society theorists, Ulrich Beck's 'risk society' struck a chord with growing popular concerns about the human and environ-mental consequences of technoscience.[24] Here science has become full of uncertainties, and is responsible for gener-ating new and unprecedented risks to society and the natural environment, whose destiny is increasingly inter-woven with our own. The promises of knowledge have been overwhelmed by the omnipresence of risk.

Once again, these new discourses of risk tend to assign change to technology itself, as if it were outside the social networks upon which it impinges. Indeed, Beck's emphasis upon de-traditionalization suggests that older, more soli-daristic social networks are being replaced by looser net-works made up of reflexively aware, but anxiety-prone, individuals. What is missing, however, is precisely an acco-unt of the new solidarities that are being created by the col-lective movements that feminism has helped to engender. In this context, it is interesting that a dominant theme of the new malestream in social theory is 'individualization' as a central feature of the 'risk society', just as these collectivities have entered the social networks of science. Indeed, the heightened public awareness of risks means that gaining public acceptance of science and technology is on government agendas everywhere. There is renewed interest in bringing non-expert citizens into participatory contact with specialists, experts and policy-makers, to create a sense of participation in risk-policy choices. Ideas of deliberative democracy are in vogue, drawing for example on models of consensus conferences and citizen juries. There is a proliferation of innovative deliberative exercises in many countries. These ideas are in tune with Haraway's call for a move away from an expert identity in science to a more democratic identity that recognizes the multiple and diverse voices of women and 'others', who are seldom heard in the conversation.[25] It is easy to understand that this may be experienced as a loss of the older certainties among previously solidary elites, but the process depends upon new solidarities and forms of agency entering to inform social and political agendas.

So it is timely that there is much debate at the moment about the way in which some feminist discourses seem to essentialize women's identity, by trying to identify commonalities in experience that could form the basis of a shared moral commitment. This is juxtaposed with a perspective that sees identities as fractured, variable and changing with context. For many, the latter position captures the truth of our postmodern condition. Yet, it also contributes to a current pessimism.[26] For is not a common identity a pre-condition for collective action? I think I have shown that this is a false opposition. We do not need to have the 'appropriate' identity prior to entering social networks; identities are formed and shaped in the manifold relations that *are* social networks. Far from this being an obstacle to feminist politics, it has been the very context in which feminist politics has flourished, linking the personal to the political, and the local to the global.

Perhaps our ideas about identity and agency remain too close to the model of solidarity and collective action proposed for the transformation of class-based industrial society, a model in which gender was conspicuous by its absence. It is doubtful that gender identities will have that form; but neither did class identities approximate their model. If the model is inappropriate, it could not describe a problem that feminism must overcome in order to be successful. Just as feminism has made a critical theoretical contribution to the understanding of science and technology as social and political, so feminist movements are among the most successful at practising 'smart' politics and shaping sociotechnical networks.

The promise of technofeminism, then, is twofold. It offers a different way of understanding the nature of agency and change in a post-industrial world, as well as the means of making a difference.

Notes

Chapter 1 Male Designs on Technology

1 Anthony Giddens, *The Consequences of Modernity* (Cambridge: Polity, 1990); *idem, The Global Third Way Debate* (Cambridge: Polity, 2001); Manuel Castells, *The Rise of the Network Society* (Oxford: Blackwell, 1996).
2 Daniel Bell, *The Coming of Post-Industrial Society* (New York: Basic Books, 1973); Alain Touraine, *The Post-Industrial Society* (New York: Random House, 1971).
3 Anne Sayre, *Rosalind Franklin and DNA* (NewYork: W. W. Norton & Co., 1975); Evelyn Fox Keller, *A Feeling for the Organism: The Life and Work of Barbara McClintock* (San Francisco: Freeman, 1983); Brenda Maddox, *Rosalind Franklin* (London: Harper Collins, 2002).
4 Autumn Stanley, *Mothers and Daughters of Invention* (New Brunswick, NJ: Rutgers University Press, 1995).
5 Ruth Oldenziel, *Making Technology Masculine: Men, Women and Modern Machines in America, 1870–1945* (Amsterdam: Amsterdam University Press, 1999).
6 Sandra Harding, *The Science Question in Feminism* (Ithaca, NY: Cornell University Press, 1986), p. 29. Harding provides an excellent map of the field of gender and science. See also Londa Schiebinger, 'The history and philosophy of women in science: a review essay', *Signs*, 12, 2 (1987), pp. 305–32.

7 Shulamith Firestone, *The Dialectic of Sex* (New York: William Morrow and Co., 1970).

8 See, e.g., Gena Corea, Duelli Klein, Jalma Hanmer, Helen B. Holmes, Betty Hoskins, Madhu Kishwar, Janice Raymond, Robyn Rowland and Roberta Steinbacher, *Man-Made Women: How New Reproductive Technologies Affect Women* (London: Hutchinson, 1985); Patricia Spallone and Deborah Lyn Steinberg (eds), *Made to Order: The Myth of Reproductive and Genetic Progress* (Oxford: Pergamon Press, 1987), pp. 34–47.

9 Rowland, in Corea et al., *Man-Made Women*, p. 78.

10 Maria Mies, 'Why do we need all this? A call against genetic engineering and reproductive technology', in Spallone and Steinberg (eds), *Made to Order*, p. 37.

11 Rachel Carson, *Silent Spring* (Boston: Houghton Mifflin, 1962).

12 See Judy Wajcman, *Feminism Confronts Technology* (Cambridge: Polity; University Park, Pa.: Penn State University Press, 1991), ch. 2.

13 Harry Braverman, *Labor and Monopoly Capital* (New York: Monthly Review Press, 1974).

14 Harriet Bradley, *Men's Work, Women's Work* (Cambridge: Polity, 1989); Ruth Milkman, *Gender at Work: The Dynamics of Job Segregation during World War II* (Urbana: University of Illinois Press, 1987).

15 Cynthia Cockburn, *Brothers: Male Dominance and Technological Change* (London: Pluto Press, 1983).

16 See n. 14 above.

17 See Wajcman, *Feminism Confronts Technology*.

18 See, e.g., Ann Oakley, *The Sociology of Housework* (London: Martin Robertson, 1974).

19 The journal *Technology and Culture* contained the first pieces on the history of domestic technology.

20 Ruth Schwartz Cowan, *More Work for Mother: The Ironies of Household Technology from the Open Hearth to the Microwave* (New York: Basic Books, 1983).

21 This is particularly evident in feminist writing on reproductive technology in the 1980s. See, e.g., Corea et al., *Man-Made Women*.

22 National Council for Research on Women, *Balancing the Equation: Where Are Women and Girls in Science, Engineering and Technology?* (New York: NCRW, 2001).

Chapter 2   Technoscience Reconfigured

1 A broad sample of the research can be found in journals such as *Science, Technology, & Human Values*; *Social Studies of Science*; and *Science as Culture*; the book series *Inside Technology* (Cambridge, Mass.: MIT Press); Sheila Jasanoff, Gerald Markle, James Peterson and Trevor Pinch (eds), *Handbook of Science and Technology Studies* (Thousand Oaks, Calif.: Sage, 1994); and Donald MacKenzie and Judy Wajcman (eds), *The Social Shaping of Technology* (Milton Keynes: Open University Press, 1985; revised and expanded edition, 1999).

2 Ruth Cowan, *More Work for Mother: The Ironies of Household Technology from the Open Hearth to the Microwave* (New York: Basic Books, 1983).

3 See Judy Wajcman, *Feminism Confronts Technology* (Cambridge: Polity; University Park, Pa.: Penn State University Press, 1991), ch. 5, for an elaboration of this point.

4 John Law, 'Technology and heterogeneous engineering: the case of Portuguese expansion', in Wiebe Bijker, Thomas Hughes and Trevor Pinch (eds), *The Social Construction of Technological Systems* (Cambridge, Mass.: MIT Press, 1987), pp. 111–34.

5 David Noble, *Forces of Production: A Social History of Industrial Automation* (New York: Knopf, 1984).

6 Cynthia Cockburn and Susan Ormrod, *Gender and Technology in the Making* (London: Sage, 1993).

7 Trevor Pinch and Wiebe Bijker, 'The social construction of facts and artifacts: or how the sociology of science and the sociology of technology might benefit each other', in Bijker et al. (eds), *The Social Construction of Technological Systems*, pp. 17–30. Interpretative flexibility does not imply that technology can be treated as infinitely plastic and tractable. The materiality of artefacts places limits on the possibilities for reinterpretation.

8 Donald MacKenzie, *Inventing Accuracy: A Historical Sociology of Nuclear Missile Guidance* (Cambridge, Mass.: MIT Press, 1990).

9 Ibid., p. 381.

10 See, e.g., John Law and John Hassard (eds), *Actor Network Theory and After* (Oxford: Blackwell, 1999).

11 John Law, 'After ANT: complexity, naming and topology', in ibid., p. 4.

12 Bruno Latour, 'Where are the missing masses? The sociology of a few mundane artifacts', in Wiebe Bijker and John Law (eds), *Shaping Technology/Building Society: Studies in Sociotechnical Change* (Cambridge, Mass.: MIT Press, 1992), pp. 225–58. Ironically, in less sophisticated hands, actor-network theory's emphasis on the agency and autonomy of material objects can itself slide into a form of technological determinism.

13 Interestingly, during the same period, the concept of 'material culture' has been restored as a core concern of social anthropology; see *Journal of Material Culture.*

14 Richard Dyer, *White* (London: Routledge, 1997).

15 Bruno Latour, 'The powers of association', in John Law (ed.), *Power, Action and Belief: A New Sociology of Knowledge?* (London: Routledge, 1986), p. 264.

16 Bruno Latour, *The Pasteurization of France* (Cambridge, MA.: Harvard University Press, 1988).

17 Judy Wajcman, *Managing Like a Man: Women and Men in Corporate Management* (Cambridge: Polity; University Park, Pa.: Penn State University Press, 1998).

18 Susan Leigh Star, 'Power, technology and the phenomenology of conversations: on being allergic to onions', in John Law (ed.), *A Sociology of Monsters: Essays on Power, Technology and Domination* (London: Routledge, 1991), pp. 25–56.

19 Bruno Latour, *Aramis, or The Love of Technology* (Cambridge, Mass.: Harvard University Press, 1996). The basic idea of Aramis was to have a train made up of small carriages which were physically separate from each other, but would combine to form a train in central parts of the network, and then split again to travel to many destinations.

20 Cockburn and Ormrod, *Gender and Technology in the Making.* See also Cynthia Cockburn and Ruza Furst-Dilic (eds), *Bringing Technology Home: Gender and Technology in a Changing Europe* (Milton Keynes: Open University Press, 1994), and Anne-Jorunn Berg, *Digital Feminism* (Trondheim: STS Centre, Norwegian University of Science and Technology, 1996).

21 Cockburn and Ormrod, *Gender and Technology in the Making*, p. 109.

22 Monica Casper and Adele Clarke, 'Making the Pap smear into the "right tool" for the job: cervical cancer screening in the USA, circa 1945–95', *Social Studies of Science*, 28 (1998), pp. 255–90; Vicky Singleton and Mike Michael, 'Actor-networks and ambivalence: general practitioners in the UK cervical screening programme', *Social Studies of Science*, 23 (1993), pp. 227–64.

23 Adele Clarke, *Disciplining Reproduction: Modernity, American Life Sciences, and 'the Problems of Sex'* (Berkeley: University of California Press, 1998).

24 This point is well made by Emma Whelan, 'Politics by other means: feminism and mainstream science studies', *Canadian Journal of Sociology*, 26, 4 (2001), pp. 535–81.

25 Nelly Oudshoorn, *Beyond the Natural Body: An Archeology of Sex Hormones* (London: Routledge, 1994).

26 This account relies heavily on Delphine Gardey, 'Mechanizing writing and photographing the word: utopias, office work, and histories of gender and technology', *History and Technology*, 17 (2001), pp. 319–52.

27 Judith Butler, *Gender Trouble* (New York: Routledge, 1990).

Chapter 3   Virtual Gender

1 Margaret Wertheim, *The Pearly Gates of Cyberspace: A History of Space from Dante to the Internet* (Sydney: Doubleday, 1999). See also David F. Noble, *The Religion of Technology: The Divinity of Man and the Spirit of Invention* (New York: Random House, 1998).

2 William Gibson, *Neuromancer* (New York: Ace Books, 1984).

3 Wertheim, *Pearly Gates of Cyberspace*, p. 259.

4 Robert D. Putnam, *Bowling Alone: The Collapse and Revival of American Community* (New York: Simon & Schuster, 2000).

5 Nicholas Negroponte, *Being Digital* (Sydney: Hodder & Stoughton, 1995); Manuel Castells, *The Rise of the Network Society* (Oxford: Blackwell, 1996); *idem, The*

Internet Galaxy: Reflections on the Internet, Business, and Society (Oxford: Oxford University Press, 2001), p. 91.

6   Negroponte, *Being Digital.*

7   Marshall McLuhan, *The Gutenberg Galaxy: The Making of Typographic Man* (London: Routledge and Kegan Paul, 1962).

8   Howard Rheingold, *The Virtual Community* (New York: Harper, 1994).

9   Castells, *Rise of the Network Society.*

10 Ibid., p. 131.

11 Castells, *Internet Galaxy.*

12 Ibid., pp. 46–7.

13 Negroponte, *Being Digital*; Rheingold, *Virtual Community.*

14 VNS Matrix, an Australian group of artists who, along with Sadie Plant, coined the term 'cyberfeminism' in the early 1990s. The group's aim was to explore the construction of social space, identity and sexuality in cyberspace.

15 Sadie Plant, *Zeros and Ones: Digital Women and the New Technoculture* (London: Fourth Estate, 1998), pp. 37–8.

16 Sadie Plant, 'On the matrix: cyberfeminist simulations', in Rob Shields (ed.), *Cultures of the Internet: Virtual Spaces, Real Histories, Living Bodies* (London: Sage, 1996), pp. 181–2.

17 Sherry Turkle, *Life on the Screen: Identity in the Age of the Internet* (New York: Simon & Schuster, 1995), p. 12.

18 Ibid., p. 314.

19 Allucquére Rosane Stone, *The War of Desire and Technology at the Close of the Mechanical Age* (Cambridge, Mass.: MIT Press, 1995), ch. 3.

20 Ruth Oldenziel, 'Of old and new cyborgs: feminist narratives of technology', *Letterature D'America*, 14, 55 (1994), p. 103.

21 Edgar A. Whitley, 'In cyberspace all they see is your words: a review of the relationship between body, behaviour and identity drawn from the sociology of knowledge', *OCLC Systems and Services*, 13, 4 (1997), pp. 152–63.

22 Plant, *Zeroes and Ones*, p. 180.

23 Anne-Marie Schleiner, 'Does Lara Croft wear fake polygons? Gender and gender-role subversion in computer adventure games', *Leonardo*, 34, 4 (2001), pp. 221–6.

24 Justine Cassell and Henry Jenkins, 'Chess for girls? Feminism and computer games', in Justine Cassell and Henry Jenkins (eds), *From Barbie to Mortal Kombat: Gender and Computer Games* (Cambridge, Mass.: MIT Press, 1998), p. 30.

25 McLuhan, *Gutenberg Galaxy.*

26 Paul Jones, 'The technology is not the cultural form? Raymond Williams's sociological critique of Marshall McLuhan', *Canadian Journal of Communication Corporation*, 23 (1998), pp. 423–54.

27 Raymond Williams, *Television: Technology and Cultural Form* (London: Fontana, 1974), p. 127.

28 Nina Wakeford, 'Gender and the landscapes of computing in an Internet café', in Mike Crang, Phil Crang and Jon May (eds), *Virtual Geographies: Bodies, Spaces and Relations* (London: Routledge, 1998), pp. 178–201; Sonia Liff, Fred Steward and Peter Watts, 'New public places for Internet access: networks for practice-based learning and social inclusion', in Steve Woolgar (ed.), *Virtual Society? Technology, Cyberbole, Reality* (Oxford: Oxford University Press, 2002), pp. 78–98.

29 Janet Wolff, 'On the road again: metaphors of travel in cultural criticism', *Cultural Studies*, 7, 2 (May 1995), pp. 224–39.

30 John Urry, *Sociology beyond Society* (London: Routledge, 2000); Bruno Latour, *Pandora's Hope: Essays on the Reality of Science Studies* (Cambridge, Mass.: Harvard University, 1999); Zygmunt Bauman, *Liquid Modernity* (Cambridge: Polity, 2000).

Chapter 4   The Cyborg Solution

1 Donna J. Haraway, *Modest_Witness@Second_Millennium. FemaleMan©_Meets_Oncomouse*™ (New York: Routledge, 1997), p. 89.

2 Ibid., p. 280.

3 Donna J. Haraway, 'A manifesto for cyborgs: science, technology, and socialist feminism in the 1980s', *Socialist Review*, 80 (1985), p. 100.

4   Donna J. Haraway, *Primate Visions: Gender, Race and Nature in the World of Modern Science* (New York: Routledge, 1989).

5   Ibid., p. 13.

6   Steven Shapin and Simon Schaffer, *Leviathan and the Air-Pump: Hobbes, Boyle, and the Experimental Life* (Princeton: Princeton University Press, 1985).

7   Ibid., p. 25.

8   See, e.g., Carolyn Merchant, *The Death of Nature: Women, Ecology and the Scientific Revolution* (New York: Harper & Row, 1980); Evelyn Fox Keller, *Reflections on Gender and Science* (New Haven: Yale University Press, 1985); Sandra Harding, *The Science Question in Feminism* (Ithaca, NY: Cornell University Press, 1986); Londa Schiebinger, 'The history and philosophy of women in science: a review essay', *Signs*, 12, 2 (1987), pp. 305–32.

9   Merchant, *Death of Nature*.

10 Harding, *Science Question in Feminism*.

11 Haraway, *Modest_Witness*, p. 22.

12 Ibid., p. 35.

13 Ibid.

14 Cris Hables Gray, 'An interview with Manfred Clynes', in Cris Hables Gray, with Steven Mentor and Heidi J. Figueroa-Sarriera (eds), *The Cyborg Handbook* (New York: Routledge, 1995), p. 49.

15 Haraway, *Modest_Witness*, p. 255.

16 *Nature*, 417 (June 2002); *GeneWatch*, UK (2002).

17 Haraway, *Modest_Witness*, p. 143.

18 Ibid., p. 47.

19 Ibid., p. 113.

20 See Paul R. Gross and Norman Levitt, *Higher Superstition: The Academic Left and its Quarrels with Science* (Baltimore: John Hopkins University Press, 1994).

21 Judith Squires, 'Fabulous feminist futures and the lure of cyberculture', in Jon Dovey (ed.), *Fractal Dreams: New Media in Social Context* (London: Lawrence and Wishart, 1996), p. 209.

22 Linda Janes, 'Introduction to Part Two: alien m/others: representing the feminine in science fiction film', in Gill Kirkup, Linda Janes, Kathryn Woodward and Fiona Hovenden (eds), *The Gendered Cyborg: A Reader* (London: Routledge, 2000), p. 92.

23 Robert Young, *Colonial Desire: Hybridity in Theory, Culture and Race* (London: Routledge, 1995).

24 Fiona Hovenden, 'Introduction to Part Four: Refractions', in Kirkup et al. (eds), *Gendered Cyborg*, p. 260.

25 Anne Balsamo, 'Reading cyborgs writing feminism', *Communication*, 10, 3–4 (1998), p. 342.

26 Brian Easlea, *Fathering the Unthinkable: Masculinity, Scientists and the Nuclear Arms Race* (London: Pluto Press, 1983).

27 Robert Jay Lifton and Greg Mitchell, *Hiroshima in America: Fifty Years of Denial* (New York: Putman's Sons, 1995), p. 19.

28 Easlea, *Fathering the Unthinkable*, p. 112.

29 Haraway, *Modest_Witness*, p. 199.

30 Michelle Matisons, 'The new feminist philosophy of the body: Haraway, Butler and Breenan', *European Journal of Women's Studies*, 5, 1 (1998), pp. 9–34.

31 Maureen McNeil, 'Techno-triumphalism, techno-tourism, American dreams and feminism', in Sara Ahmed, Jane Kilby, Celia Lury, Maureen McNeil and Beverley Skeggs (eds), *Transformations: Thinking Through Feminism* (London: Routledge, 2000), p. 230.

Chapter 5 Metaphor and Materiality

1 Jane Millar and Nick Jagger, *Women in ITEC Courses and Careers* (London: Women and Equality Unit, DTI, 2001). See also the US National Science Foundation.

2 Although there are significantly more women in software programming in developing countries such as India, Mexico and the Philippines, here too they are scarce at higher levels.

3 See Judy Wajcman, *Feminism Confronts Technology* (Cambridge: Polity; University Park, Pa.: Penn State University Press, 1991), ch. 6. See also Wendy, Faulkner and Maria, Lohan (eds), 'Men, masculinities and technologies', *Men and Masculinities*, 6, 3 (forthcoming 2004).

4 Judy Wajcman, *Managing Like a Man: Women and Men in Corporate Management* (Cambridge: Polity; University Park, Pa.: Penn State University Press, 1998).

5 Cynthia Cockburn, 'The material of male power', in Donald MacKenzie and Judy Wajcman (eds), *The Social*

Shaping of Technology: Second Edition (Milton Keynes: Open University Press, 1999), p. 181.

6 See, e.g., Elizabeth Grosz, *Volatile Bodies: Toward a Corporeal Feminism* (Bloomington: University of Indiana Press, 1995); and the journal *Body and Society.*

7 'New robot face smiles and sneers', *New Scientist*, 17 February 2003.

8 See Lucy Suchman, *Plans and Situated Actions: The Problem of Human–Machine Communication* (Cambridge: Cambridge University Press, forthcoming). For a more positive feminist reading of the new forms of embodiment suggested by intelligent robots, e.g., see Claudia Castañeda, 'Robotic skin: the future of touch?', in Sara Ahmed and Jackie Stacey (eds), *Thinking Through the Skin* (London: Routledge, 2001), pp. 223–36.

9 See the series of conference proceedings of the 'Women, Work and Computerization' group of the International Federation of Information Processing (IFIP): e.g., Kea Tijdens, Mary Jennings, Ina Wagner and Magaret Weggelaar (eds), *Women, Work and Computerization: Forming New Alliances* (Amsterdam: North-Holland, 1989).

10 Michael Bittman, James Rice and Judy Wajcman, 'Appliances and their impact: the ownership of domestic technology and time spent on household work', *British Journal of Sociology*, forthcoming.

11 See *http://architecture.mit.edu/house_n.*

12 Anne-Jorunn Berg, 'A gendered sociotechnical construction: the smart house', in MacKenzie and Wajcman (eds), *Social Shaping of Technology*, pp. 301–13.

13 Michael Bittman and James Rice, 'The Spectre of Overwork', *Labour and Industry*, 12, 3 (2002), pp. 5–25. In the growing service economy, much of the labour is indeed provided by other less affluent women.

14 'Third-wave' and 'postfeminism' are both expressions currently widely used in North America to distinguish the contemporary moment in feminist thinking and practice from the earlier period of second-wave feminism. See Ann Braithwaite, 'The personal, the political, third-wave and postfeminisms', *Feminist Theory*, 3, 3 (2002), pp. 335–44.

15 Saskia Sassen, 'Towards a sociology of information technology', *Current Sociology*, 50, 3 (2002), pp. 365–88, at

p. 381. For a more sceptical view, which questions the assumption that giving subaltern women access to telecommunications is necessarily emancipatory, see Gayatri Chakravorty Spivak, 'Claiming transformation: travel notes with pictures', in Sara Ahmed, Jane Kilby, Celia Lury, Maureen McNeil and Beverley Skeggs (eds), *Transformations: Thinking Through Feminism* (London: Routledge, 2000), pp. 119–30.

16 Sassen, 'Towards a sociology of information technology'; see also Robin Mansell, 'From digital divides to digital entitlements in knowledge societies', *Current Sociology*, 50, 3 (2002), pp. 407–26.

17 For example, Coltan is implicated in the civil wars in the Democratic Republic of Congo and Rwanda that are usually assigned to 'ethnic conflict', and thus seen as remote from Western lives. See UN Security Council Report of the Panel of Experts on the Illegal Exploitation of Resources and Other Forms of Wealth of the Democratic Republic of the Congo, 12 April 2001, listed on the web site of the Mineral Resources Forum (*http://www.natural-resources.org/minerals/law/conflict.htm*). The severe food shortages that this has given rise to have forced people to seek bush food, thereby threatening the local population of gorillas and raising serious environmental concerns. In a postmodern twist, fans of Leonardo Di Caprio can join a letter-writing campaign to support the gorilla population at his web site as part of his commitment to environmental awareness.

18 See Wajcman, *Feminism Confronts Technology*, pp. 74–8.

19 Barbara Ehrenreich and Dierdre English, *Witches, Midwives and Nurses: A History of Women Healers* (Old Westbury, NY: Feminist Press, 1973).

20 Steven Epstein, 'Democracy, expertise, and AIDS treatment activism', in Daniel Kleinman (ed.), *Science, Technology, and Democracy* (Albany: State University of New York Press, 2000), p. 20.

21 UNAIDS web site.

22 See *Social Studies of Science*, 26, 2 (1996).

23 For an excellent discussion of these issues, see Emma Whelan, 'Politics by other means: feminism and mainstream science studies', *Canadian Journal of Sociology*, 26, 4 (2001), pp. 535–81.

24 Ulrich Beck, *Risk Society* (Cambridge: Polity, 1986).

25 From the perspective of technofeminism, however, debates about new forms of scientific governance remain framed in too limited terms. The rhetoric of risk assessment imposes on citizens the responsibility to grasp the science rather than requiring scientists to be transparent in their practices. There is also the fundamental question of the limited range of technologies that citizens may deliberate between. Democratic participation in technological politics has hardly penetrated the decision-making structures of research and design. Innovation, design and the interests that drive them, not just the consequences of technoscience on society, should be matters for democratic deliberation. While it is crucial for women to take their rightful place in the discursive or meaning-making processes of technoscience, we also need to influence the powerful institutional forces that shape upstream innovation trajectories.

26 This helps to explain why postmodern feminists have been sympathetic to cyberfeminist accounts of new technologies. They seem to provide a way out of pessimism by sidestepping the problem of the common identity thought necessary as a pre-condition for collective action.

Index

LaVergne, TN USA
16 September 2010
197065LV00010B/2/P